THE A

KINGDOM OF GOD

The Awesome Kingdom of God

In Plain Sight

Afc, Paul Vickers

The Awesome Kingdom of God

'In Plain sight'

ISBN: **978-0-9600947-2-1**

ISBN: **978-0-9600947-2-1**

Library of Congress Control Number:

Registration #: TXU2142092

Print information available from:

Published date: August 31st 2019

Table of content

Introduction

Greetings in the unparalleled name of Jesus the Christ who is God's only **begotten** Son. My purpose for writing this book stems from Godly ardent desire to see Ephesians 4:13 fulfilled in my lifetime. "***Till we all come unto the unity of the faith and of the knowledge of the son of God unto a perfect man unto the measure of the stature of the fullness of Christ***." From my meetings with pastors, educators, schools, Bible teachers, I realize we are not all on the same page of understanding God's Word to the degree we are able to convey the same message to those whom we meet on a daily basis.

"***That there should be no schism in the body; but that the members should have the same care one for another***." I Corinthians 12:25. Schism is a split or division between strongly opposed sections or parties, caused by differences in opinion or belief. A Biblical term which has been absent today is the word **commonwealth**. The Word of Truth confirms, "***And the multitude of them that believed were of one heart and of one soul: neither said any of them that ought of the things which he possessed was his own; but they had all things common***." Acts 4:32. Beloved, the word **individualism** has quickly risen and taken over which is now more prevalent than ever before. Everyone seems to be only looking out for number one.

Let us heed God's pin-pointed directive to seek the Kingdom so that we can finally grow together as one effective organism in The Lord and do exploits again in Jesus name. Most believers are still looking to earth's government to solve their problems in the hope for a better tomorrow. However, we will only experience a positive change if we maintain a Godly lifestyle and acknowledge Him in all our ways. "…***But you are a chosen generation, a royal priesthood, a holy nation, His own peculiar people, that you may proclaim the praises of Him who called you out of darkness into His marvelous light.***" 1 Peter 2:9. Our potential is **un**imaginable if we embrace His Word.

There are (23) Key and Major Topics Which We Will Be Addressing and Answering.

The introduction of these (23) pin-pointed questions below will be covered in great details using only Scriptural references. Also, this outline is designed to start-out with a simple rendition of God's awesome administration. However, the subjects are not in the same pattern but they will be revealed as you read through "**The Awesome Kingdom of God.**" Enjoy the reading and unveiling!

What is a kingdom?
Where is The Kingdom?
What is the Gospel of God?
Is the Gospel The Kingdom?
Who heads-up The Kingdom?
What did Jesus bring to earth?
What is The <u>Key</u> of Knowledge?
How do you enter The Kingdom?
What are the <u>Keys</u> of the Kingdom?
How many <u>Keys</u> of The Kingdom are there?
What are the nine Blessings of The Kingdom?
When did The Kingdom of God arrive on earth?
The Kingdom of God and Jesus' second coming!
What are the four ways The Holy Spirit is received?
Is the Holy Spirit a Person & does He speak audibly?
Is there a particular message the enemy comes to steal?
What is the difference between Jesus' baptism and John's?
Is there a difference between being sealed and being filled?
What is it The Father does for us which greatly pleases Him?
What are the nine gifts of the Holy Spirit that Paul mentioned?
What did Paul preach at the beginning and end of his ministry?
Jesus said, "I appoint unto you a Kingdom." What did He mean?
The difference: The Kingdom of God and The Kingdom of Heaven?

Chapter I
The Right Outlook & New Mind-frame In the Kingdom

You are about to see some things your eyes may have never seen; you are about to read sequence of words you may have never read. And, you are about to realize more of the magnificent workings of the things pertaining to the awesome Kingdom of God which is in plain sight. Evidence of God's brilliance was concealed but brought back to earth by Jesus approximately 2,000 years ago. The imprint of His glory and majesty are still evident today which is what we are about to unfold!

Let us begin by asking you a stunning and thought provoking question. 'What is it that God the Father does for you which greatly pleases **Him?'** God's Word tells us, "***do not fear, little flock, for it is your Father's good pleasure to give you the kingdom***." Luke 12:32. What an eye-opener! Could there be such a thing where the giver – **God**– is more pleased than –you– the receiver; not possible! Yet, this is true and accurate as well as the extent God went to just for you! What exactly does this mean?

First, the administration Jesus brought is headed-up by His Holy Spirit; He is the **Holy Spirit**-not holy-~~ghost~~- whose operation and infilling revolutionized the works of Jesus and all the apostles. God gave them someone who could provide healing to the world and God in-turn would get the glory. Is it crystal clear that God wants to equip His saints with His Spirit which will please Him? Yes, when we choose to allow God to take up residence in us, it pleases Him.

Secondly, do you remember on several occasions when healing was done; once by "…***the shadow of Peter passing by might fall on some of them***? Acts 5:15. The other by the Apostle Paul? "***And God wrought special miracles by the hands of Paul***:" Acts 19:11. God's Word clearly states, "***of a truth I perceive that God is no respecter of persons***" Acts 10:34. Finally, God's Holy Spirit can still empower and equip believers today to provide restoration to others and expel disease. People today are destitute and desire to be free of oppression, incurable disease, drug addiction and cancer. As we grow and increase in proper knowledge it should result in a change in our direction, mind-set and approach. God is waiting on us; yet, we are sitting back waiting on Him! As ministers, we are the ones to affect the world and improve the lives of all those within our sphere of influence. God does have a presence here on earth; who is it, **you**!

Again beloved, the first and most critical component which should be changed towards God is our mind-set. This is what the word 'repent' means. If we never change the way we think, we will never change the way we are! "***For as he thinks in his heart, so is he..."***. Proverbs 23:7. One of the things we have to rid ourselves of is a servant's mindset so that we can embrace either a steward's outlook or, an ambassador's assignment. We are about to detail just five (5) of the more than fifteen of these characteristics below.

An ambassador is also a steward of an entire country. Every other title or designation mentioned in Scripture about us pale in comparison. Why, because of its governmental role and assigned responsibilities. Did you know the only one of more than sixty titles in The New Treaty directed to believers that the Apostle Paul identified himself with that of an ambassador? ***For which I am an ambassador in bonds: that therein I may speak boldly, as I ought to speak***." Ephesians 6:20. Even though he used others, he held this one above the rest. Let us now delve into only the top five characteristics of an ambassador;

1st **Represents Jesus** in all they do in the world. ie:-------→'offspring'
2nd Elected official of the **highest rank**. ie--------rep Heaven to earth
3rd **KNOWS their constitution** ie:----------------→The Word of God
4th **NEVER** state personal opinions but:ie---"my gov'ts position is.."
5th MUST **make peace** where ever they go. ie:-------→this is priority!

If we do not take His directives seriously right now as stewards, we will never impact lives around us and those who desire to receive more from God. God desire us to carry out His mandates which goes far beyond any world titles or standards. As children of the day, we are also the light of the world according to Jesus and therefore, someone is always seeing your light wherever you go. "…***you are the light of the world***." Matthew 5:14. The Word of Life says regarding His Disciples, "***and He opened their understanding, that they might comprehend the Scriptures***." Luke 24:45. As citizens of Heaven on earth, we are here to provide answers because we understand who we are in God which can make a huge difference in the lives of everyone around us. In other words, we are difference makers!

As you may be aware, the Word of God has clearly identified the number one problem with humans. Scientists and psychologists too have conducted their independent research and the conclusions they arrived is the same which the Word of Life mentioned over six thousand years earlier. Both conclusions landed at the same destination which is **identity crisis**.

In conjunction with both conclusions, there are five great questions of life *–below–* which God's Word answers. We believe these are man's greatest problems. Let us personalize it so that it really leaves an indelible mark in your transformed mind. The left side asks the questions and the right side provides the Biblically correct answers.

1--Who **<u>are</u>** you?--------This is related to your real **<u>identity</u>** with God
2--Where did you **<u>come from</u>**?-----From above; this is your **<u>heritage</u>**
3--Why are you **<u>here</u>**?-----------God will reveal to you, your **<u>purpose</u>**
4--What can you **<u>do</u>**?--------You are **<u>limitless</u>**; all things are **<u>possible</u>**
5--Where are you **<u>going</u>** when you die?--------→ This is your **<u>destiny</u>**

<u>First</u>, is our **<u>identity</u>**; our life is hid with Christ in God and we are to also be called 'sons of God.' "***Behold, what manner of love the Father has bestowed upon us that we should be called sons of God***." I John 3:1. Also, "***but as many as received him, to them gave he power to become the <u>sons of God</u>***." John 1:12 This addresses who we really are from God's vantage point; women are also sons!

<u>Secondly</u>, is our true **<u>heritage</u>** which is not just of earthly parentage because it is from a Heavenly origin. This means God knew you would

ıere you are today, living where you live and looking
’ He knew you would. Do you remember when Jesus finished teaching about the kingdom in the synagogue? They asked, "***is not this the carpenter's son***...? Matthew 13:55. Jesus declined and mentioned His heritage instead which was not of earth's parentage, as follows; "***I am from above. You are of this world; I am <u>not</u> of this world."*** John 8:23.

<u>**Thirdly**</u>, Jesus knew specifically why He came to earth and what His <u>**purpose**</u> was; it was to bring in a new administration to earth. The first one needed to be upgraded. "***Then indeed, even the first covenant had ordinances of divine service and the earthly sanctuary***." Hebrews 9:1 "***But now He has obtained a more excellent ministry, inasmuch as He is also Mediator of a better covenant, which was established on better promises."*** Hebrews 8:6.

<u>**Fourth**</u>, asks the questions, 'what can we do.? We are <u>**limitless**</u>! "***Jesus said to him, "If you can believe, <u>all things are possible</u> to him who believes***." Mark 9:23. Never before was this statement mentioned about any saint in the Old Testament. You see beloved, this proclamation is letting all believers in Christ know what they are now capable of from the least to the greatest.

"<u>Finally</u>, there is laid up for me the crown of righteousness, which the Lord, the righteous Judge, will give to me on that Day, and not to me only but also to all who have loved His appearing." II Timothy 4:8. Again, God's Word provide us with history as well as a current status and future with Him. In other words, you have a:

Real	**identity**
Godly---------------------------→	**heritage**
Definite	**purpose**
You are without----------------→	**limits**
And, you have a Certain	**destiny.**

These characteristics are only realized if we acknowledge Him in all our ways and make godly choices along the way in our daily lives.

God can always provide answers to His offspring the same way parents can offer solutions for their children's situations.

At times during my one-on-one meetings, I frequently ask people a very short three-word question which is relevant to be the single greatest question of life we mentioned earlier; it is, "**<u>who are you</u>?"** Before they begin to answer, I add a pre-qualifier by stating, **"but you can't give me your name or your occupation**?" I have asked this of many people in all walks of life and professions. For the most part, the majority struggled because they use their occupation to define themselves.

The majority of 'Christians' all defaulted to, "<u>well, I am a child of God</u>." However, my follow-up question to them, "**is that what you said when someone asked you, 'who are you,' or did you give them your name/profession?"** We are spending quality time in this area because it is the only launch-pad from which we are able to ascend to the upper stratosphere in God and see ourselves from His vantage point. We are never to let what we do define us! Now let's look at this same question from a whole new perspective. If, in fact, adults struggle in this area, then what do you think our young people would say?

Without proper knowledge, our young people will land in the arena of confusion and inquire of someone other than their Source –**God**– to define themselves. Therefore, if we **don't** know who we are or where we are going, any road will take us there! On the other hand, if we have proper focus, and know why we are here, then life will be detailed and **<u>not</u>** about experimentation and error but fulfilling our Godly purpose. Also, if this 'three-word question' is not addressed early and properly, we will begin to hurt and use others to get what we want.

This is why the Word of Life prioritizes our ultimate directive. "***But seek first the kingdom of God and His righteousness and all these things shall be added unto you.***" Matthew 6:33. Once we separate personal goals from Godly requirement, it should catapult us into a realm of an outstanding relationship with the Godhead. As His off–

spring, we are to throw away the old traditions and grab hold of the new mind-set, no matter how we feel or what others tell us.

This is why we have to grow in knowledge of God and who we really are by not embracing the low mindset of a "servant." If we hold-on to servant, we would be making **Jesus** a 'king of servants,' not "**King of kings**!" "***And He has on His robe and on His thigh a name written: KING OF KINGS AND LORD OF LORDS.***" Revelation 19:16.

Again, "***But as many as received Him, to them gave He power to become the sons of God, even to them that believe on His name.***" John 1:12. The proper knowledge we secure early in life is designed to equip some of us later-on to judge angels as well as the world. "***Do you not know that the saints will judge the world***?" Also, "***Do you not know that we shall judge angels? How much more, things that pertain to this life?***" I Corinthians 6:2-3.

In addressing this seemingly concealed subject matter of "**The Awesome Kingdom of God,**" it is what we are to vigorously pursue and seek to find out more about this breathtaking empire. According to God, we are now identified with Christ and are children of light. This is why the Word says, "***And because you are sons, God hath sent forth the Spirit of his Son into your hearts, crying, Abba, Father.***" Galatians 4:6. Finally, we "…***were sealed with that Holy Spirit of promise.***" Ephesians 1:13.

Defining The 'Kingdom' of God

First and foremost, the word kingdom is derived from two words, **king** and **domain**. The word **king** means ruler and **domain** is a territory. When you combine them, they spell out a very **un**familiar word, king-domain. In the English language, we like to abbreviate/shorten words; this is how we arrived at **kingdom**.

A kingdom therefore, is an area or territory governed by a king. You cannot be a king without having a domain/territory. We know the reigning King to be none other than, **Jesus the Christ**. How did He become King? He was born **King**! Matthew 2:2. Jesus ruled His domain of earth approximately 2,000 years ago; then, He took things a step further and showed His Disciples how to rule! The Word of Life confirms and says, "***Most assuredly, I say to you, he who believes in Me, the works that I do he will do also...***" John 14:12. After Jesus demonstrated and exercised His Heavenly authority on earth for three and one half (3 ½) years, He decided to delegate this same ability/governance to anyone who would choose to follow Him.

The only condition was *–and still is–* if they use His name to exercise their legal rights as citizens of Heaven on earth. As saints, we have been given delegated authority over sickness, disease, oppression and over both the devil and demons. As you know, the enemy is called satan, and 'the god of this world' system but not over us as God's offspring.

Jesus said, "***And as you go, preach*** –proclaim– ***saying, 'The Kingdom of Heaven is at hand.***" Matthew 10:7. Jesus did not come to bring a religion but an administration which would impact born again believer's lives. Again, He came to be our example and to demonstrate what humans are capable of doing as children of the Most High. ***"But when the multitudes saw it, they marveled, and glorified God, which had given such power unto men."*** Matthew 9:8. It is now your opportunity to get on-board with His Holy Spirit.

The First of (3) Definitions of The Kingdom

The first of three definitions surrounding the kingdom will be spelled out in extremely great detail. The kingdom of God is His **invisible** administration which was on earth at the time of creation between 6,000-7,000 years ago. Therefore, according to the Word of Truth, the earth is NOT millions/billions of years old according to history books and scientific discoveries which they erroneously theorized.

A very simple but profoundly sound answer is that the original rulership of earth was headed-up by God's Holy Spirit. After Adam and Eve relinquished earth to the fallen Cherub called Lucifer, who then became satan; God's Holy Spirit *–who managed earth since its creation–* had to leave because of the change in administration. You see beloved, The Holy Spirit was not going to remain on earth under satan's jurisdiction. Again, when someone believes and confess Jesus as Lord, the Holy Spirit will return to take up residence back on earth in believers to seal them. This is why the Word says, "***you were sealed with the Holy Spirit of promise.***" Ephesians 1:13. The Holy Spirit will place His mark on every convert to identify them as God's property; they become His temple where He rules as Lord. See I Corinthians 6:18. Jesus said, "***Behold, I give unto you power to tread on serpents and scorpions, and over ALL the power of the enemy: and nothing shall by any means hurt you***." Luke 10:19.

In essence, even though satan is the god of this world system, believers are given authority in his territory as long as we remain in proper alignment, exercise their rights as citizens and use the mighty and matchless name of Jesus. "***And whatever you do in word or deed, do all in the name of the Lord Jesus, giving thanks to God the Father through Him.***" Colossians 3:17.

Throughout the upcoming chapters as well as verses like; **Prov. 3:5-6, Acts 8:37** and **Rom. 10:9-10**, we would like to point out, whenever you read the word "**HEART**" please apply it as follows:

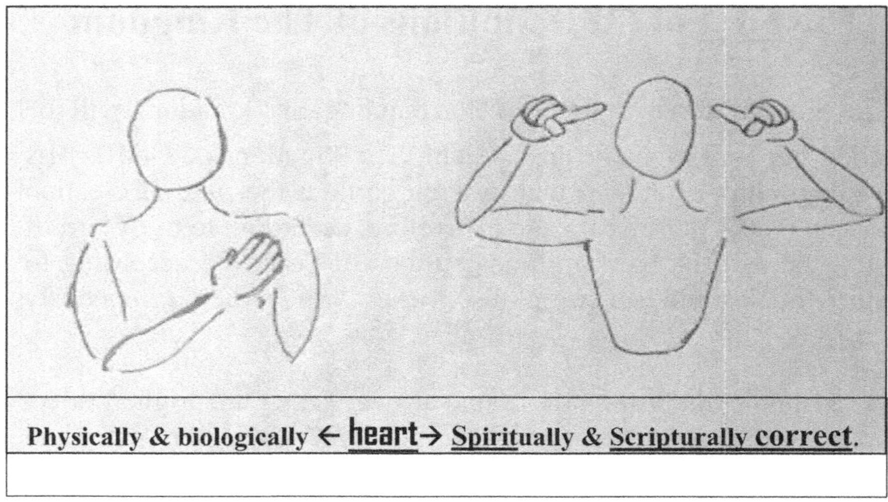

Physically & biologically ← heart→ Spiritually & Scripturally correct.

The Second of (3) Definition of The Kingdom

The second definition is also today's description of the **invisible** kingdom of God since the time God clothed as human *–Jesus the Christ–* walked on earth. The Word of Eternal Life says, "***The law and the prophets were until John: since that time the kingdom of God is preached, and every man presses into it.***" Luke 16:16. As we know, there was a time limit for the Law of Moses which ended when John was arrested, put in prison and taken out of the way.

Jesus' administration *–led by the Holy Spirit–* picked up where John's ministry ended. John's assignment was to herald-in/announce the arrival of the Ultimate King. Beloved, it was Jesus who brought the administration of God to earth. This means, the baton was passed from the fore-runner *–John–* to "***…the author and finisher of our faith…***" Hebrews 12:2. This is Jesus who is King of kings! God's Kingdom is an entire administration as seen on the illustration below.

The left side consist of earth's government and the right side represents the Heavenly administration right now. However, the right side shows the huge distinction and superior spiritual nature using the same nine (9) characteristics the world adopted. They are:

Earthly Gov't ---------------------- **God's Heavenly Gov't on Earth**

Admin, Governor, Pres, PM's ---- The Head person; **The Holy Spirit**
Army -------------------- not believers in Christ but the **angels** of God
Ambassador -----------We now **represent** the Ultimate Leader/Jesus
Citizens ------------------- must become familiar with our legal **rights**
Constitution ----- Governing & fundamental principles **live by**: Bible
Culture ------------- obey **customs**/proper lifestyle ie: forgive & love
Economy $$ ---------(occupation) $$ Tithe, offering, vow and giving
Language -----------communication, **converse**/speak in mystery; pray
Laws--------------------- system created to **regulate/punish behavior**

Every *–major–* country on earth is unique; yet, there are at least nine (9) main commonalities among all of them. Again, on the left side, we list what both country's characteristics comprises of; on the right are the stunning features we as citizens in this kingdom of God realize today. As we know, it was the prophet Isaiah who first saw that The Messiah would be bringing an entire governmental administration to earth which would leave a permanent imprint forever. You only make changes to bring in something new or if the old system was outdated and needed replacement. How about, it was just not measuring–up to its expectation; isn't that true? Let's prove it.

The prophet Isaiah said, "***For unto us a child is born, unto us a son is given: and the government shall be upon his shoulder: and His name shall be called Wonderful, Counsellor, The mighty God, The everlasting Father, The Prince of Peace. Of the increase of His government and peace there shall be no end***.". Isaiah 9:6-7.

In essence, the most profound and complete description of the kingdom of God is: "**God's invisible administration that Jesus left on earth to be governed by His Holy Spirit. We enter through 'the Door' to be born-again and are given keys to access/operate it as Stewards of God who are also Ambassadors for Christ. We become citizens who reflect the King's culture, nature and holy lifestyle to the world.** We will include only ten (10) of many other supporting scripture verses which support our findings and paint an enormous detailed picture. It is painted as follows:

God's **invisible government** which Isaiah saw 400 years' prior that The Messiah's arrival 2,000 years later which He would be bringing to earth. –Isaiah 9:7– It is administered by the **Holy Spirit** –I Corinthians 12:7–. We enter through the Door/**Jesus** –John 10:9– to be **born–again** –John 3:3,5, I Peter 1:23– and are given **keys** – Matthew 16:19– to access/operate it as **Stewards** of God. –Luke 16:2– We become **Ambassadors** –II Corinthians 5:20– for Christ and **citizens** –Philippians 3:20– who obey and reflect the King's **culture** and **nature**–I Peter 1:16– and **lifestyle** to the world. –Matthew 5:16– As we are now made aware, the only administrator of earth's territory is none other than His Awesome Holy Spirit.

He is:

The Spirit of **God**:--**Genesis 1:2**
The Spirit of **Christ**--**Romans 8:9**
and **He is** The 'Spirit of **Truth**' ----------------------------**John 16:13**
Again, the Holy Spirit is the only person who Jesus left to manage the distribution of gifts to all God's Offspring on earth as He sees fit. **See John 16:7 and I Cor. 12:11.**

The Third and Most Astounding Definition of the Kingdom

The final description of the Kingdom of God is brilliantly spelled out in several unique ways. First, it is expressed in stunning details by both Jesus and John in the last book in the Word of God which is "**The Revelation of Jesus Christ**." The territory John describes in this unveiling is God's eternal **visible** governmental administration which is what Jesus went back to Heaven to prepare for His coming.

This statement was confirmed by Jesus when He said, "***Let not your heart be troubled; you believe in God, believe also in Me. "In My Father's house are many mansions, if it were not so, I would have told you. I go to prepare a place for you. And if I go and prepare a place for you, I will come again and receive you to Myself; that where I am, there you may be also."*** John 14:2.

This physical kingdom is a massive construction project of epic proportion which Jesus has been working on for two millennials; it will be making its debut when He brings it to earth. This radiant and brilliantly lit city by the **glory** of God *–who is Jesus Christ Himself–* is a cube/square city of transparent gold which is between 1,200 – 1,500 miles **high**, **long** and **wide**. Jesus will be setting-it up on the earth as a permanent habitation for both God and man called the **New Jerusalem**. Today, saints of the Most-High know this "**city of peace**" to be the **New Jerusalem**. By the way, **Jeru** means city; **Salem** means peace. This is stunning and overwhelming information to fathom and conceive. Again, the New Jerusalem is a spectacular city of **crystal**

clear gold, minted with the most dazzling and priceless gemstones from its colossal foundation to its soaring pinnacle. The walls consist of twelve foundations; each of which are constructed out of a different and precious gem. Most people have never grasped its magnificence with its streets of transparent gold; its structure has four sides and three monumental gates of great pearls on each side.

Beloved, what you are about to envision is simply spectacular, amazing and impressive. Never before has this sequence been spelled out in such vivid detail of God's ultimate dwelling-place on earth. God did give David *–a king in the Old Testament–* a glimpse of this extraordinary and brilliant city. He said it has eternal attributes, marvelous functions and glorious majesty of what this kingdom will be like. King David commentary was as follows:

1.. ***The LORD is good to all, and His tender mercies are over all His works***
2..***All Your works shall praise You, O LORD,***
3..***And Your saints shall bless You***
4..***They shall speak of the glory of Your kingdom,***
5..***And talk of Your power***
6..***To make known to the sons of men His mighty acts,***
7..***And the glorious majesty of His Kingdom***
8..***Your Kingdom is an everlasting Kingdom,***
9..***And Your dominion endures throughout all generations."***

Psalms 145:9-13.

Now, in the book of the Revelation of Jesus Christ, John describes it in more spectacular and intricate details what this great city is like. It is as follows; ***"And the building of the wall of it was of jasper: and the city was pure gold, like unto clear glass. And the foundations of the wall of the city were garnished with all manner of precious stones.***

The first foundation was jasper;
the second, sapphire;
the third, a chalcedony;
the fourth, an emerald.
The fifth, sardonyx;
the sixth, sardius;
the seventh, chrysolyte;
the eighth, beryl;
the ninth, a topaz;
the tenth, a chrysoprasus;
the eleventh, a jacinth;
the twelfth, an amethyst.

21 And the twelve gates were twelve pearls: every several gate was of one pearl: and the street of the city was pure gold, as it were transparent glass.

22 And I saw no temple therein: for the Lord God Almighty and the Lamb are the temple of it.

23 And the city had no need of the sun, neither of the moon, to shine in it: for the glory of God did lighten it, and the Lamb is the light there-of. Revelation 21:18-23.

Presently, as dual citizens of earth and God's administration, we realize that the first thirteen verses in Genesis there is light but no sun. And, in the last twenty-six verses of Revelation, there is also light but no sun. How fascinating this is to imagine and conceive! There was God before He created the sun; yet, there was light; and, there is God in the New Jerusalem; yet, there will be no sun!

Most of us are looking forward to finally living outside-of time. This why when the angel flew by he said, "...***that there should be time no longer***." Revelation 10:6. We live in time but that is about to change very soon. This magnificent city of transparent gold is where we will be spending eternity *–outside of time–* with Our Father God and Lord with Jesus the Christ. Please begin to focus more on the book of the Revelation of Jesus Christ because there is even a special and added blessing for reading, hearing and keeping those things in mind. "***Blessed is he that reads, and they that hear the words of this prophecy, and keep those things which are written therein: for the time is at hand***." Revelation 1:3.

Everyone wants to go and live in Heaven and yet, God wants to come to live with us by bringing His spectacular and magnificent kingdom/administration to His renovated earth. Another stunning and remarkable facet about what the earth will be like is as follows; "***And I saw a new Heaven and a new earth: for the first heaven and the first earth were passed away; and there was no more sea***!" Revelation 21:1. Our most universal substance will be no more! God's monumental structure will be able to be seen from any geographical location on the planet because of its unprecedented height!

What will be the primary message proclaimed in God's marvelous and spectacular kingdom? The answer to this question has probably never been accurately addressed or properly taught in seminaries, churches or Bible study sessions across the globe. Beloved, we are referencing the **'everlasting gospel'** mentioned by John in the book of Revelation. He said, "***And I saw another angel fly in the midst of heaven, having the everlasting gospel to preach unto them that dwell on the earth, and to every nation, and kindred, and tongue, and people***." Revelation 14:6.

As we know, the word 'gospel' means **Good News**; the good news is the Kingdom of God which was brought back to earth by Jesus which Isaiah saw. **Isaiah 9:6-7**. In the Old Treaty, it was primarily about God; in the New Testament, it details Jesus The Christ. In the New Jerusalem it will be about God's awesome Holy Spirit. "***And the Spirit and the bride say, "Come!" And let him who hears say, "Come!" And let him who thirsts come. Whoever desires, let him take the water of life freely***." Revelation 22:17. The message which will be declared is the kingdom dynamics. This is why the Word of Life says we are to study, grow, increase and live a holy lifestyle every day. God wants us fully equipped with His Word, use the keys He left us and look forward to eternal life in His stunning physical kingdom.

Chapter II
Who Heads-up This Marvelous Kingdom?

The answer to this direct question above is one of the most spectacular unveiling throughout the entire Doctrine of The Lord. While Jesus was here physically, He made profound and startling statements about Himself and the arrival of His Holy Spirit; "***Nevertheless I tell you the truth; It is expedient for you that I go away: for if I go not away, the Comforter will not come unto you; but if I depart, I will send Him unto you***." John 16:7.

As you have read, Jesus was heading back to the right hand of His Father but He was also sending the **Holy Spirit** -not holy ~~**ghost**~~- in His place; He would be in charge, preside over and distribute the nine (9) gifts only to born-again believers. When we properly define His 'Holy Spirit' by words; the word **'Holy'** means '**one**' or, **set apart**.' The word '**Spirit'** *–as pertaining to **Him**–* when we combine both words; they reveal and describe Him precisely as, the; "**One**"

S-pecial
P-erson
I-nspired *to*
R-each
I-nstruct &
T-each

Jesus always referred to the Holy Spirit as a person. **See John 14:26**. Later on, Luke mentioned that He gave clear instructions and did so assertively or calmly depending on the situation. For example, God's Holy Spirit spoke to the Apostles as follows:

"then The Holy Spirit **said** to Phillip, go near---------------- Acts 8:29
"while Peter thought about the vision the Spirit **said** ------ Acts 10:19
"the Spirit **told** me to go with them without hesitation ---- Acts 11:12
"As they worshipped the Lord…the Holy Spirit **said**-------- Acts 13:2
"**forbidden** by The Holy Spirit to preach the word in Asia -- Acts 16:6

All who believe and confess Jesus as Lord, the first assignment His Holy Spirit carries out is to **seal** each believer with God's mark of identification. And, He continues to do so, even today. "...***after that you believed, you were <u>sealed</u> with that Holy Spirit of promise***." Ephesians 1:13. The Holy Spirit does **NOT** fill everyone right away; even though He can; His first work is to place His mark of ownership on each believer who accepts Jesus as Lord/owner. Again, the Apostle Paul further confirms. ***"And, grieve not the Holy Spirit of God, whereby you are <u>sealed</u> unto the day of redemption.***" Ephesians 4:30.

As you can see above, the Holy Spirit **teaches**, **speaks**, **distributes** and **seals** believers because He manages **<u>all</u>** facets of the kingdom. The Apostle Paul used the framework of a building to convey yet another very fascinating feature about Jesus. This building he uses consist of having nine (9) levels/stories accessible using nine (9) keys. We know that God is the **<u>Builder</u>**; Jesus is the **<u>Door</u>** into this building and His Holy Spirit is the **<u>Administrator</u>** of the building.

The Gospel of God clearly confirms all of the above in great detail. "***Now, therefore, you are no longer strangers and foreigners, but fellow citizens with the saints and members of the <u>house</u>hold of God, having been <u>built</u> on the <u>foundation</u> of the apostles and prophets, Jesus Christ Himself being the chief <u>cornerstone</u>, in whom the whole <u>building</u>, being <u>fitted</u> <u>together</u>, grows into a holy <u>temple</u> in the Lord, in whom you also are being <u>built</u> <u>together</u> for a <u>dwelling place</u> of God in the Spirit***." Ephesians 2:19-22.

Notice the relevant association of all the underlined words to that of a construction. Now, as far as the world is concerned, Jesus mentioned the works His Holy Spirit does as well; He said, "***and when He is come, He will reprove*** –convict– ***the world of sin, and of righteousness, and of judgment***." John 16:8. Beloved of God, the Holy Spirit is on assignment here on earth by Jesus to reach, instruct and teach believers. He will convict **<u>un</u>**believers of their alien status which are not in-line with God's directive. Let us address yet another important question; do we pray to the Holy Spirit? No, we petition the Father in Jesus name but acknowledge His Holy Spirit as the power source to seal, fill, guide and provide insight. How do we receive the

Holy Spirit? There are at least **four ways** mentioned in Scripture whereby we can receive His awesome power and infilling.

First, Jesus said, "…***how much more shall your heavenly Father give the Holy Spirit to them that ask him?"*** Luke 11:13. Again, God's Holy Spirit's first assignment is to seal everyone, not to fill them. Ephesians 1:13. However, He can do both at the same time!

Secondly, "…***And when He had said this, He breathed on them, and said to them, "receive the Holy Spirit***." John 20:22.

Third, "***And when Paul had laid hands on them, the Holy Spirit came upon them, and they spoke with tongues and prophesied***." Acts 19:1-(**6**) Acts 8:14-(**18**).

Fourth, Paul said, "***and we are His witnesses to these things, and so also is the Holy Spirit whom God has given to those who obey Him***." Acts 5:32. These four verses are simply amazing and require memorization for retention and meditation in order to secure them! In all aspect of life, God's Holy Spirit can be received.

Is There A Particular Message The enemy Comes to Steal?

As a child of the Most High, you are about to read Jesus' most astonishing statement ever made to saints about the enemy. It requires an attentive ear and laser beam focus which we are **NEVER** to overlook or lose sight of. Not only did Jesus fully expose the enemy, He told us the **only** time he will show up for any event. Jesus said, "***When any one hears the word of the kingdom, and understands it not, then cometh the wicked one, and catches away that which was sown in his heart***…" Matthew 13:19.

Stunning; the enemy does not send his demons to steal this extremely valuable message but he shows up personally to try and hopefully steal this exclusive treasure from those who are slow to understand the kingdom dynamics. Why would he only steal one message? The answer is; it is the **ONLY** one which lets believers know of their legal rights, who they are in the spirit realm, the authority they possess and what they can do about the enemy's works. Are we understanding the magnitude of what The Word says and who we really are?

Did Jesus really spell out to us that there is no other message throughout God's Word whereby the enemy *–personally–* is interested? Jesus, do you mean; the cross, love, the resurrection, salvation, eternal life, Heaven, prosperity, baptism, religion and anything else we could think of does **not** appeal to the enemy as does the kingdom? **YES!**

This is exactly what Jesus was specifically getting us to grasp, realize and be conscious of. Now do you see why we are placing such a great emphasis on knowing 'The Awesome Kingdom of God.' The enemy knows that only God's kingdom *–**not** religion–* can expose his deceptive works. This is the only thing he's afraid of! As stewards of God and ambassadors for Christ, His Holy Spirit teaches us all things, unveils this spiritual truth and distributes the nine (9) gifts mentioned in 'I Corinthians 12' as He sees fit.

Finally, the Holy Spirit discloses/provide keys which accesses and operates God's Kingdom. Therefore, as a child of God, if you have keys, you become the **key** yourself. Beloved, the key to life is God; the key to success is edifying yourself which locks-out the enemy's influence. We provided a great acronym which unveils a very powerful step to success.

K-eep
E-ducating
Y-ourself

This is how we access revelation of God. Beloved, if you were the enemy and hate humans, wouldn't you steal their Crown Jewels?

God's Gov't/Administration is Clearly Seen

The Word of Truth says, "***For since the creation of the world His invisible attributes are clearly seen, being understood by the things that are made, even His eternal power and Godhead, so that they are without excuse,***" Romans 1:20. This means, we do not know all there is to know yet. However, we are to strive and desire to know more about the **God-Head**, especially about His Holy Spirit who presides over this kingdom and all of God's works in the lives of His stewards.

Jesus said, "***but if I with the finger of God cast out devils, no doubt the kingdom of God is come upon you.***" Luke 11:20. Also, in the Word of Life, it spells out in detail what the kingdom does **not** entail and what it actually encompasses. "***For the kingdom of God is not meat and drink...***" Romans 14:17. Next, the Apostle Paul points out, "***for the kingdom of God is not in word...***"I Corinthians 4:20. In other words, this invisible but real kingdom/administration of God is here on earth but it is **not** about the following three (3) things;

1–Meat
2–Drink
3–Neither in word

As offspring, when we take a closer look at the underlined words, we see that the kingdom of God is **not** about festivities, drink or words. God's Word provides us with more detailed information about this new administration which Jesus brought and taught throughout His ministry. Now let's read what this administration is primarily about: ***for the kingdom of God is not in word but power.***" I Corinthians 4:20. Again, "***For the kingdom of God is not meat and drink but righteousness, peace and joy in the Holy Spirit.*** "Romans 14:17. Here, in plain sight we are given the specific details what it is about:

1 –Power
2 –Righteousness
3 –Peace
4 –Joy

Now that we are given precise details about God's awesome administration, let's see what is required as citizens. Remember, Jesus said we have two directives; we are to **seek** after the kingdom and to keep ourselves properly aligned in **right standings** with Him and His teachings. "***But seek first the kingdom of God and His righteousness and all these things shall be added unto you***." Matthew 6:33. Again, these are Jesus' two priorities for all citizens. Also, as ambassadors for Christ we are given additional mandates and promises. There are some saints who realize God's invisible kingdom is on earth and its magnificence envelops these four (4) main characteristics; **power, righteousness, peace** and **joy** in His Holy Spirit. The diversity of God's Holy Spirit is evident but His works seem to confuse some mature saints.

When we closely examine the Doctrine of The Lord, we marvel at all that is spelled out about God's Holy Spirit. God does not want us to go down the road of popular beliefs, personal opinions and **not** seek revelation of Him for authenticity or accuracy. There is a relevant passage in Scripture where it pinpoints the difference of being **sealed** and being **filled** by Him.

"***And it happened, while Apollos was at Corinth, that Paul, having passed through the upper regions, came to Ephesus. And finding some disciples,***

2 he said to them, "Did you receive the Holy Spirit when you believed?" So they said to him, "We have not so much as heard whether there is a Holy Spirit."

3 And he said to them, "Into what then were you baptized?" So they said, "Into John's baptism."

Then Paul said, "John indeed baptized with a baptism of repentance, saying to the people that they should believe on Him who would come after him, that is on Christ Jesus."

When they heard this, they were baptized in the name of the Lord Jesus. And when Paul had laid hands on them, the Holy Spirit came

***upon them, and they spoke with tongues and prophesied*.**" Acts 19:1-6. As you have just read, there are two distinct kinds of baptisms. See also Matthew 3:11. The question is, what are you going to do about them? As the body of Christ, we are part of a Heavenly administration here on earth and we know that only:

1--citizens have	**rights**
2--stewards have----------------------------→	**responsibilities**
3--ambassadors are given	**assignments**.

Let us ask you this simple but obvious question; are you a member of the United States or, are you a citizen? Beloved, do you see why it is important to see yourself as a citizen of God's kingdom and not members of a church? Anyone who comes into a country illegally does not have the same rights and privileges as citizens of that country. Therefore, only citizens today in the kingdom of God are clothed with **righteousness** –II Cor. 5:21– in the New Treaty ~~not filthy rags~~ as spelled out in the Old Treaty saints by Isaiah in 64:6.

Today, we are expected to walk uprightly before man so that God gets the glory. This is why the Word of God says, "***Let your light so shine before men, that they may see your good works and glorify your Father in Heaven*.**" Matthew 5:16. Did you know that **<u>no one</u>** in the Old Covenant was continually righteous before God? As a matter of fact, we just read that God considered man's righteousness as filthy rags. Again, "***And all our righteousness are like filthy rags...***" Isaiah 64:6. However, now it says "***For He made Him who knew no sin to be sin for us, that <u>we</u> might become the righteousness of God in Him*.**" II Corinthians 5:21. What they lacked yesterday, we have today!

A Child's Insight of The Kingdom

Over the past several years, I have asked many people a simple and direct question regarding the late night meeting with Jesus and Nicodemus. The question is; the encounter between Nicodemus and Jesus was about what…? Invariably, the answer defaults to that of being born again which is not accurate! The session was **<u>not</u>** about birth but primarily about how to **enter** the kingdom. Born again was Nicodemus' focus; the kingdom was Jesus' emphasis. When my daughter was sixteen years old, I was speaking to her about the encounter between Jesus and Nicodemus. In the middle of unveiling my magnificent find, she interrupted me and said, "I get it, I get it!" I mentioned to her that I was not finished explaining!

Again, she boldly declared, "I get it, I get it!" I looked at her and said, go ahead, tell me what you think you get! Actually, I was expecting her to say something off-base and inaccurate so I could correct her misunderstanding. However, this was not the case! The words which came out of this teenager were not only profound but filled with insight, clarity and revelation. She said, "the meeting was not about being born again, but how to get into the kingdom of God."

Jesus was addressing the destination and process but Nicodemus was focusing only on birth. My daughter went on to explain, 'I am here – *home*– and my school is over there *–eight miles away–* which is the destination; "**born again is the road I travel to get to my school which is to "the kingdom"**'! I was speechless, stunned and taken-back with this marvelous unveiling. Not only did she "steal my thunder" but it showed me God is still revealing to our young people relevant information.

And, He will continue to provide them with insight if they simply listen to what God will reveal to them. Hundreds of years earlier in the Old Treaty, the prophet Joel mentioned this distribution and unveiling. He said, "***and it shall come to pass afterward that I will pour out My Spirit on all flesh; Your sons and your daughters shall prophesy, Your old men shall dream dreams, Your young men shall see visions***." Joel 2:27. The title 'sons' is only for us in the New Treaty. I mentioned to my daughter, every time I teach this encounter, 'going forward' I will mention your explanation and revelation. Also, I mentioned to my wife *–as Jesus stated–* "***out of the mouth of babes and suckling, thou has perfected praise.***" Matthew 21:16. I learned a great lesson in 2014 about youths; they are listening to what we teach them even when we do not think they are paying attention.

When Did The Kingdom Of God Arrive & **How** Do We Enter Its Brilliance?

The answers to this combined question is the most critical of all subjects to address. Most people would like to know specifically the answer to both **when** did the kingdom arrive and **how** do we enter its region. Let's dive right into the two most prevalent examples which Jesus mentioned. First, "***And He said to them, assuredly, I say to you that there are some standing here who will not taste death till they see the kingdom of God present with power.***" Mark 9:1.

As it is spelled out, God's administration was present at the time of Jesus ministry; He clearly told us, there are people right in His presence who will not die before they experience and perceive its magnificence. Next, Jesus said, "***But if I cast out demons with the finger of God, surely the kingdom of God has come upon you.***" Luke 11:20. In other words, the authority to expel demons is another clear indication that another government more powerful is present.

This awesome power and authority of the kingdom of God was **not** coming at some point in the future because Jesus brought it with Him to earth! Remember how the people, "...***marveled, and glorified God, which had given such power unto men.***" Matthew 9:8. And, it is why Isaiah said, "...***of the increase of His government and peace there will be no end...***". Isaiah 9:7. In other words, there is no end or limitation to this new administration and it will come with **peace** which passes all natural understanding. This **peace** means 'the absence of frustration.' This Scripture verse above simply confirms what Isaiah prophesied hundreds of years earlier which was being fulfilled right before their eyes.

Also, this administration would be vivid enough so that its impact would be in plain sight and an obvious reality. In essence, it was not something God was hiding but chose to reveal. As a result of its presence, Jesus gave the religious lawyers a very stern warning! "***But woe to you, scribes and Pharisees, hypocrites! For you shut up the kingdom of heaven against men; for you neither go in yourselves,***

nor do you allow those who are entering to go in. ” Matthew 23:13. The word ‘**woe**’ means hardship, sorrow or distress. How enlightening is this statement! Again, Jesus clearly pointed out that the religious lawyers were fully aware of its presence and impact but they deliberately prevented the people from entering its splendor.

This is what really angered Jesus because those who knew better were withholding the ticket, solution and answer which the people desperately needed in order to change their lives! Secondly, "***when He was asked by the Pharisees when the kingdom of God would come, He answered them, "The kingdom of God does not come with observation. Nor will they say, 'Here it is!' or 'There it is!' For remember, the kingdom of God is within*** –among– ***you.***" Luke 17:20-21.

This means you do not go to a church to be in the kingdom because it is right where you are; it is through believing and confessing Jesus as Lord/owner of your life and living according to His guidelines. God revealed to Isaiah that an entire government would be arriving with The Messiah. Now let us address how we enter God's marvelous domain/kingdom on earth. First, Jesus said, "***But as many as received Him, to them He gave the right to become children of God, to those who believe in His name.***" John 1:12.

Upon this confession, our spirit is born again which is mentioned in John 3:3-5, I Peter 1:23 and '**sealed**' –Ephesians 1:13– by His Holy Spirit. These are specific step-by-step actions which we must choose to take in order to experience and enter its splendor. Therefore, once someone believes and confess Jesus The Christ as Lord, they are entitled the right to be called both sons of God and ambassadors for Christ. By the way, angels were called 'sons of God's in the Old Treaty. However, in this New Treaty, believers own this title and status.

Then, the Apostle Paul confirmed just how we are rescued and brought into the kingdom. He said, "***that if you confess with your mouth the Lord Jesus and believe in your heart that God has raised Him from the dead, you will be saved.***" Romans 10:9. As a steward, you know the access, entrance or admission into any physical building or event is usually through a door. Again, Jesus disclosed exactly who He is in relationship to this access. John confirmed, ***"I am the Door. If anyone enters by Me, he will be saved, and will go in and out and find pasture."*** John 10:9. Jesus was clearly stating, there is an administration present; there is only one way in and 'I Am the key you need.' This is both a stunning statement and a highly exclusive right. Almost every religion today and belief of tomorrow will have a problem accepting this single and monumental statement.

Now we are about to read that Jesus took His message to an even higher plateau by stating what it takes mentally for anyone to enter spiritually into this glorious domain. He said, ***"Whosoever therefore shall humble himself as this little child, the same is greatest in the kingdom of heaven."*** Matthew 18:4. Humility therefore is one major qualifier for entrance into His kingdom along with our belief and confession. Beloved, as we all know, we do not enter a new company and carry any degree of arrogance but a state of humility.

Did you know, humility happens to be one of the **nine keys** of the kingdom of God. Its modesty is so important to the kingdom dynamics that, Jesus said, "***And whoever exalts himself will be humbled, and he who humbles himself will be exalted***." Matthew 23:12. Question, is this verse telling us that God wants to exalt those who choose to humble themselves? Precisely!

This is exactly what is being conveyed in a crystal clear format. How about Peter's perspective about humility? He says, "***Therefore, humble yourselves under the mighty hand of God, that He may exalt you in due time***." 1 Peter 5:6. Your invitation for God to exalt you has arrived at your address right now! And, God is awaiting your response to His offer so that you fulfill your part of the contract. The question is, will you open the package and sign the 'offer letter' so that God can begin to exalt you?

Qualifications & New Titles Once We Enter the Kingdom

Jesus, in The New Testament was the Person of **God** in The Old Testament; He provides us with the very first detailed description of the qualification of how to enter the kingdom. It is critical to reiterate that He said, you "**MUST be born again**" to enter God's kingdom. Again, John 3:3-5. In God's kingdom, we are recognized as either a steward, a wise person *–because you win souls (Proverbs 11:30) to Christ–* or, an ambassador for Christ because we are all given detailed responsibilities to fulfill where ever we go. Only the world sees us as Christians which means followers of Christ.

Remember, Jesus never referred to anyone as a Christian but sons of God, friend, stewards, light of the world, salt of the earth and many more titles. There are over ten other titles Jesus assigned to everyone who chooses to follow Him. As a matter of fact, we would like to point out that there are three main outlooks which we should all be aware of. **First**, there is God's view of how He sees us; **then**, there is the world's view of us. **Finally**, there is the way we are to see ourselves.

1st- **God's** view of you is	**Wise**	Prov. 11:30
2nd-The **world's** view of you is a:	**Christian**	Acts 11:26
3rd-**You** are to see yourself as a:	**Steward**	Luke 16:2

Each of the above varies widely yet, all three are stunningly accurate. As far as any of the other titles are concerned, they are all significant based on our surrounding and activities. I love asking questions, not to test someone but only to observe answers. Two of my favorite are, "**as a Christian, what do you do**?" The other is, "**as an ambassador or steward, what are your assignments**?"

We are to be keenly aware of what God sees when He looks at us! Again, when the world looks at you, they ID you as a Christian. "***...and the disciples were first called Christians in Antioch***." Acts 11:26. What were they called previously? They were called **saints** or those of **The Way**! Acts 24:14.

Again, the answer behind the questions are to bring about the right identification and full awareness of what is God's standard. God wants us to see ourselves as representing Jesus to the world just as ambassadors represent one country to another. "***Now then, we are ambassadors for Christ...***" -II Corinthians 5:20. Also, as a steward. "***As each one has received a gift, minister it to one another, as good stewards of the manifold grace of God.***" I Peter 4:10. Why would the Word of Life use a title like steward to describe us and to address us as ambassadors for Christ?

Do you think the Holy Spirit instructed holy men/writers to use these words liberally? Below, both titles, '**steward**' and ambassadors will be spelled out in very unique acronyms side-by-side. They are designed not just to define their roles but to aid and implant the responsibilities they convey as well.

As we know, in the Hebrew language, the name of a person or thing represents the thing; and, the thing is the name. Acronyms, sometimes referred to as theological anthologies *–when used to spell-out terms relating to deity–* enhance the meaning as well. We constantly reference both these terms throughout this book because they share certain high responsibilities. Both of these words/titles spell out:

S-omeone	**A**-ssigned
T-o	**M**-any
E-ntrust	**B**-asic
W-ith	**A**-reas *of*
A-ffairs	**S**-tewardship
R-esponsibilities *and*	**S**o
D-uties	**A**-ctual
	D-uties
	O-utweigh
	R-ituals

As you can vividly see, a steward's responsibilities are interrelated with an ambassador's role. And, they do not involve rituals or traditions of old. Remember on our worldly job how we had directives and responsibilities to adhere and follow on a daily basis? These two titles above are directives which we are to embrace and carry-out regularly. As far as making peace and loving one another are concerned, they were and still are our directive. "...***see that you love one another with a pure <u>heart</u> fervently***." 1 Peter 1:22.

Comprehensively, loving is one thing; doing so fervently and sincerely is on a whole other level! Could you imagine if all believers fulfilled just the first five responsibilities of an ambassador on page **#2**. As you recall, the Apostle Paul identified himself as an ambassador. "***For which I am an ambassador in bonds***..." Ephesians 6:20. Again, believers in Christ today are to be called stewards of God –**Luke 12:42**– and ambassadors for Christ; **II Cor. 5:20.**

Jesus said, we are also '**the light of the world**.' We live at the pinnacle of reward, favor and obtain constant revelation by His Spirit of Truth. The Holy Spirit is our teacher, revealer of truth and disclose hidden truth about the **God–Head**. As stewards, we have directives to follow in order to stay aligned with the windows of Heaven.

One of the primary instructions given is that of **forgiveness** which should be an immediate response and not an after-thought reaction. "***So likewise shall my heavenly Father do also unto you, if you from your hearts forgive not everyone his brother their trespasses***." Matt. 18:35 And, as offspring, we consciously know there are higher standards which we live-by than those in the world because we know someone is always watching. People are jealous of you and haters are waiting for us to slip-up and fall. Therefore, live intentionally for God.

Two of the deadliest toxins some mature believers still carry should be flushed down the toilet immediately; they are **<u>slander</u>** and **<u>malice.</u>** Slander can be speaking the truth about someone that is **<u>not</u>** necessary to mention. Malice or shunning is what some groups do today to brothers and sisters if they dare leave their organization. These destructive practices will sever both the lines of communication with the Holy Spirit as well as hinder blessings they are entitled to receive from God when they walked in proper alignment. Furthermore, these two deviations above, are **<u>iniquities</u>** which are worse than **<u>sin</u>**! We will address the severity of iniquity compared to sin a little later.

Chapter III
What Would Cause You to Sell All You Possess?

It is very interesting to ponder or even contemplate on the above titled question. Most people's immediate response would be either, I would never sell or give up all I have for anything! Or, if someone considers, they may conclude, it would have to be something unimaginable or of epic proportion. In Jesus' address concerning both the value and magnificence of the kingdom of God, He said, ***"again, the kingdom of heaven is like treasure hidden in a field, which a man found and hid; and for joy over it he goes and sells all that he has and buys that field."*** Matthew 13:44.

Immediately following one example, Jesus provided yet another stunning account. ***"Again, the kingdom of heaven is like a merchant seeking beautiful pearls, who, when he had found one pearl of great price, went and sold all that he had and bought it."*** Matthew 13:46. What a great extent Jesus went to; just to wake them up to the extreme value of the kingdom, its prominence and its wealth!

Nowhere else in Scripture is the kingdom presented in such magnitude using comparative analysis to bring to light the scale and greatness of its value. In other words, sell everything and get this one thing! Or, discard your religious direction and seek His kingdom as you would hid treasures! Let's further review the sequence above.

First, Jesus mentions an extremely valuable prize that is found; then, there was consideration of its magnitude. Next, the founder made a wise business decision to purchase. Notice that both examples used extreme sacrifice of personal possessions to obtain just **one** gem. Also, notice its worth which is of higher importance and greater in value and significance than everything he owned. On yet another occasion, Peter had the audacity to represent the rest of "Team Jesus" *–the disciples–* and let Jesus know, "...***See, we have left all and***

followed You. So He said to them, Assuredly, I say to you, there is no one who has left house or parents or brothers or wife or children, for the sake of the kingdom of God, who shall not receive many times more in THIS present time, and in the age to come eternal life. Luke 18:28-30.

Please continue to meditate, grab ahold and chew-on Jesus' three (3) stunning words, "***many times more***!" In Mark's writing, he stated, "***hundredfold***..." Mark 10:30. Now let's digest it all slowly! You see beloved, Jesus had laser-beam focus and a primary message which He brought to deliver; He did so with a sense of urgency for the entire three and one half years of ministry. Only few mature believes are aware of the greatness, accessibility and worth of this marvelous administration.

Did you know, there were one hundred–forty (140) common people who Jesus authorized besides His Disciples to cast out demons, heal the sick and cleanse disease? See Luke10:1. Jesus' intent was to demonstrate there is power available through Him in this new administration which He brought. This way, those who recognized God's power would shift the focus from religious dead works of that day to embrace God's governmental authority done by their friends and colleagues. Jesus' intent was to greatly impact the present generation as well as generations to come two thousand year later.

Beloved, Jesus paralleled His administration vs personal treasures which everyone could easily identify with, make a clear choice and enjoy something far superior. As we have and will mention numerous times, Jesus said, ***"But seek first the kingdom of God and His righteousness, and all these things shall be added to you."*** Matthew 6:33. Please read the entire fifth and sixth chapters to familiarize yourself with what those '**things**' are! They provide great detail and a whole new insight into God's work and abundance! Again ambassadors, the Administrator, Governor and leader of this entire regime is His Awesome Holy Spirit. Why are we to pursue this kingdom; because everything we need today is in one place! Remember, Matthew referred to it as the '**key** of knowledge.' Let's enthusiastically pursue the kingdom as we would hidden riches!

Is There A Difference Between the Gospel and The Kingdom?

In our quest to define, disclose and detail both the underlined subjects, we will provide you with precise examples of what God's Word says about the Gospel is as it relates to the kingdom. Again, the word 'Gospel' means '**Good News.**' The Good News is that the "**kingdom of God**" has returned to earth again. As we mentioned earlier, this statement may be contrary to what most believers may have heard taught that the 'gospel' is the death, burial and resurrection of Jesus.

This seems true but it is NOT accurate! If Jesus' demise was good news, did John the Baptist mention it? It would stand to reason that if John was His fore-runner, then he would provide insight and prepare the people. However, he did **no** such thing! Also, it is interesting to note that only after John the Baptist was arrested and put in prison, did Jesus begin to present the kingdom. Let's prove it; "***Now after John was arrested, Jesus came into Galilee, proclaiming the gospel of God, and saying, "The time is fulfilled, and the kingdom of God is at hand; repent and believe in the gospel."*** Mark 1:14-15.

In essence, the Old Testament is now fulfilled; John was taken out of the way so that Jesus could usher in this new and explosive administration headed-up by His Holy Spirit. Again, the Gospel or Good News of God's kingdom governance is what the Prophet Isaiah saw approximately four hundred years prior to Jesus bringing this new administration on His **shoulder.** What was He carrying to earth for man to access and experience? It was the greatest news for all humans!

As we stated before, ***"...And of the increase of His government and peace, there shall be no end.*** " Isaiah 9:7. Again, the kingdom is God's government on earth right now which is presided over solely by His Awesome Holy Spirit who is the Person of God in-charge. And, He, "...***distributes to each one individually as He*** –determines– ***wills***." 1 Corinthians 12:7-11. As you know, there are nine (9) gifts which He alone supervises and does so exclusively to those who have confessed Jesus as Lord. See Romans 10:9-10. These gifts are given **only** as He deems, not when we ask for the one we desire! The Holy Spirit will reveal/bestow a gift(s) depending on our situation when He sees it appropriate. See **Mark 13:11**. However, this is contingent upon our continual righteous lifestyle and close communion with Him.

More Compelling Insight About the Gospel

"***And Jesus went about all Galilee, teaching in their synagogues, and preaching the gospel of the kingdom, and healing all manner of sickness and all manner of disease among the people***." Matthew 4:23. Beloved, the gospel is not a stand-alone message but a combined one. Again, the 'Gospel' means '**Good News**' which goes hand-in-hand with something else which is The Kingdom.

"…***unlike Moses, who put a veil over his face so that the children of Israel could not look steadily at the end of what was passing away. But their minds were blinded. For until this day the same veil remains unlifted in the reading of the Old Testament, because the veil is taken away in Christ***." II Corinthians 3:13-14. As a steward, what you are about to read is simply astounding. Did you know, "…***the strength of sin is the law***?" I Corinthians 15:56.

Furthermore, "***for what the law could not do, in that it was weak through the flesh, God sending his own Son in the likeness of sinful flesh, and for sin, condemned sin in the flesh***." Romans 8:3. And, as we mentioned earlier, "***But now He –Jesus– has obtained a more excellent ministry, because He is the Mediator of a better covenant, which was established on better promises***." Hebrews 8:6. Do you really think the enemy wants his plans to be exposed to believers in Christ and established into the minds of the general public?

As a reminder, we know the enemy comes **ONLY** to steal one message. Again, this would be the Crown Jewels of life and spiritual unveiling to everything in life which is none other than the awesome Kingdom of God. What is the evidence! "***When anyone hears the word of the kingdom, and does not understand it, then the wicked one comes and snatches away what was sown in his heart.***" Matthew 13:19. Only God's kingdom can expose and destroy any other kingdom! As stewards, we know there is God's priority and our personal pursuit. Which one are we to choose? Some saints are **not** aware that we are to proclaim the kingdom's arrival everywhere we go. Jesus stated in Matthew 10:7, "***As you go, preach saying the kingdom of God has arrived.***" The Holy Spirit will work with those who have confessed Jesus as Lord to guide them on how to exercise their delegated authority, heal the sick, cast out demons, cleanse the leper, raise the dead, cure disease, cast evil spirits out of people and resist him! **Luke 10:19**. With eyes wide open, we have been given the right to conduct spiritual business everywhere on God's physical earth!

The Kingdom of God and Jesus' Second Coming

The "**Gospel**" or "**Good News**" of the kingdom is the only message Jesus said we are to mention as we minister to others. Therefore, we are to become very familiar with the characteristics of the kingdom and its operations. This message is so critical that Jesus mentioned it as the only sign which will precede His second coming. "...***and this gospel of the kingdom shall be preached in all the world for a witness unto all nations; and then shall the end come.***" Matthew 24:14. What an eye–opener!

Remember, Jesus told us He was leaving but He was coming back. "***And if I go and prepare a place for you, I will come again, and receive you unto myself; that where I am, there you may be also***." John 14:3., since Jesus is returning to earth, then we should find out exactly what sign will pave the way of His arrival, wouldn't you agree? This way, we can discipline ourselves and choose to live a holy lifestyle "***because it is written, be holy, for I am holy***." I Peter 1:16. As saints, we also know the type of church He will be coming back to receive. The Gospel of God says, "***that He might present it to Himself a glorious church, not having spot, or wrinkle, or any such thing; but that it should be holy and without blemish***." Ephesians 5:27. As of today, we are to ask ourselves two monumental questions:

1 - **Do I know what the kingdom is and its keys of operation?**
2 -**Am I announcing the right message whenever I speak?**

The right answers are that we should declare and speak about the things pertaining to the Awesome Kingdom of God which is now being revealed to you in plain sight. Do you remember when the people asked Jesus, where is this kingdom that He was always making reference to? He said to them, "...***For the Kingdom of God is already among you."*** Luke 17:21. Beloved, He brought it but it was invisible!

Remember, Jesus said to His Disciples and those whom He sent out, "***And as you go, preach*** –proclaim– ***saying, 'The kingdom of heaven is at hand."*** Matthew 10:7**.** This message was received then. However, it is NOT taught in today's churches as Jesus' mandate. We have substituted what we feel are more important subject matters like; water baptism, three ways to prosper, tithe and offering, the cross, the crucifixion, lovers of self, ten (10) things to success, the devil, two kinds of faith, being salt and light, four (4) ways to build strong faith and a host of other seemingly good topics. However, Jesus said we are to "...***seek first the kingdom of God and His righteousness***..." (Matt. 6:33) which encompass authority including His second coming!

The Difference Between the Kingdom of <u>God</u> and the Kingdom of <u>Heaven</u>

These days, there seems to be so much confusion as to the difference between the Kingdom of God and the Kingdom of Heaven. However, there is a simple yet profoundly sound distinction that should clear all/any rubble of confusion. The Kingdom of Heaven is '**the seat of God's authority**' where He rules right now. The Kingdom of God is on earth where the Holy Spirit has jurisdiction in the lives of believers; Again, He alone distributes the nine (9) gifts mentioned by Paul. Beloved, the church is the agency or out-post of Heaven. Anyone who believes and confess Jesus as Lord becomes both **citizens** of the kingdom of God and **members** of the body of Christ; not members of a church.

Therefore, the church represents the local government's head-office. As citizens in His outpost, we are called stewards, heirs and ambassadors for Christ. By the way, did you know that **ONLY** Matthew mentions the Kingdom of Heaven? Also, we must point out that Matthew used both terms interchangeably. Every other writer **only** used the kingdom of God where Matthew uses the kingdom of Heaven concerning the same subject matter. Please check and verify!

It is widely believed the reason Matthew used Kingdom of Heaven is that he was a Jew. His writing was done in a way they would readily receive the message in this style/format. We are never to get hung up on terms but rely on the Holy Spirit for truth, insight, clarification and revelation. This is His job, respectfully speaking! Again, the kingdom of God is an administration which God put in place to take over what was old and no longer effective.

As you know, it was revealed to the Prophet Daniel when he stated, "***Then the kingdom and dominion, And the greatness of the kingdoms under the whole heaven, shall be given to the people, the saints of the Most High. His kingdom is an everlasting kingdom, and all dominions shall serve and obey Him."*** Daniel 7:27. This description is referencing believers in Christ Jesus today who are heirs of salvation and ambassadors for Christ.

Knowing the Difference between Kingdom and Religion

A simple turn-key and natural definition of a kingdom is an administration governed by a king. My finding is similar to that of the early to Heaven, Dr. Myles Munroe. The definition of a Kingdom is, **"the governing influence of a king over his territory; impacting it with His will, purpose and intention; creating a citizen of people who reflect the king's culture, nature and lifestyle**." Also, a **KING**dom is God's design; religion is man-made! Later on, we will provide even a more detailed description along with corresponding scripture to further substantiate the impressiveness of a kingdom.

It is important to note that a king is always responsible for his citizens/subjects in his domain as well as for their well-being. Here in the United States, it is extremely difficult to acknowledge a '**kingdom**' perspective because we live in a democratic/republic and are independent thinkers who are divided people by ethnic groups, religion, color and opinions. According to our political views, there are no absolutes in the world we live because everything is debatable.

"*There can't be just one way*" but many because we are diverse in all we do. However, God's Word clearly opposes what we think; it says, "***till we all come in the unity***..." Ephesians 4:13. We dispute and differ on almost everything the government does and institute as law. On the other hand, in a kingdom everything the king says becomes instant law without debate, a hearing, dispute or question. In defense of the King James Version of God's Word, the scholars who interpreted the scrolls and **transliterated** it; they did so under the penalty of death for any errors deliberately made.

Today, this is not the case with some other translations. The love of money and diversity are the main players. Did you know that the king in a kingdom is also called **Lord?** This word or title means **owner**! The king owns absolutely everything in his kingdom. This includes the water, the trees, the birds, your dog, your cat, the food, your children, your wife, your husband, your car and anything else you could think of. Blessed of The Lord, are you now seeing '**kingdom**' in a whole new light both vertically and horizontally?

Back in the Old Treaty, there is a profound example of both Lordship and priesthood which clearly shows recognition and a detailed understanding of both. We are referencing Sarah's address to her husband Abraham. Did you know, she called him **Lord**? I Peter 3:6. Why would a wife acknowledge her husband as lord? The reason is that Sarah was smart and understood when she used the title Lord, she was letting him know that he is responsible for her; this includes her well-being as well as being her provider and protector.

As children of the **Most-High**, this is exactly the weight and aura it carries when we call Jesus Lord; it means He is responsible for us, our situation and owns our body because His Holy Spirit dwells there. "***Or do you not know that your body is the temple of the Holy Spirit who is in you, whom you have from God, and you are not your own?" For you were bought at a price; therefore, glorify God in your body and in your spirit, which are God's.*** 1 Corinthians 6:19-20. As heirs of God, our own body does not really belong to us!

Now, let's accurately and precisely provide a definition of religion. It can be viewed as, "**a set of fundamental beliefs agreed upon by a group of people that use rituals, ordinances and traditions to govern their affairs; there is usually a founder or person** *–or governing body or, inner circle–* **at the helm. The members exalt, adheres to and obeys their 'ruling body' <u>even if</u> it is contrary to God's established Word.**

Also in a religion, they can vote to make changes, adjust as they see fit and modify things for the overall benefit of their organization; as long as it does not interfere with their by-laws and mission statement. Most of what is written in God's Word is used but just a little toxin mixed in! It is like a glass of water with a drop of poison. Man-made religion is totally opposite and contrary to a kingdom which is a theocracy and requires God's standard to be maintained regardless!

Therefore, religion and the kingdom of God have nothing in common. For example, let's visit a very familiar series of scripture. As a steward of God who has been made the righteousness of God in Christ, we cannot amend, adjust vote-on or change anything in the constitution to suit ourselves or specialty group's chosen lifestyle. It is what has been written in God's Word which is always the standard.

"***For I am the LORD, I change not***." Malachi 3:6. It is no secret that one major church body has adjusted God's Word to suit a particular lifestyle in order to retain members and stop the precipitous cash flow that was walking out the door. There is no president, prime minister, pastor or even an angel who should add or take away from anything written in God's Word. "***But though we, or an angel from heaven, preach any other gospel unto you than that which we have preached unto you, let him be accursed***." Galatians 1:8.

Also, "***For I testify to everyone who hears the words of the prophecy of this book: If anyone adds to these things, God will add to him the plagues that are written in this book. And, if anyone takes away from the words of the book of this prophecy, God shall take away his part from the Book of Life, from the holy city, and from the things which are written in this book."*** Revelation 22:18-19. This should serve as both a major deterrent as well as a stern warning. Woe unto you!

Beloved, what you are about to read is both shocking and enlightening. "***And He*** –Jesus– ***said unto them, verily I say unto you, there is no man that hath left house, or parents, or brethren, or wife, or children, for the Kingdom of God's sake, who shall not receive manifold more in this present time, and in the world to come life everlasting***." Luke 18:29-30.

As Jesus was teaching the multitude, someone stopped Him because His mother and siblings were outside desiring to speak with Him. The way He responded seemed to head in a totally different direction. Jesus spelled-out that real estate, job, family, relatives/kin, marriage and children are **not** on the same plateau to God as does The Kingdom message. There are multiple things you are yet to receive.

Today, it is widespread that there is nothing more important than family. Well, according to Jesus there is something much more valued and prized; it is the Kingdom dynamics. Maybe this is why He stated, ***"but seek first the Kingdom…"*** Matthew 6:33.

Beloved, Jesus clearly outlined the superiority, extreme worth and awesome attributes linked to The Kingdom. In other words, if there is a choice between going after possessions/wealth, job, family, husband/wife or children, put them second and choose/seek to become familiar with The Kingdom first because there is much more attached! I think you will agree, the take-away from Jesus' account is that we need to change our priority, shift the focus, revamp our daily calendar and appointments so that it reflects The Kingdom. It is far deeper than we can imagine because it even has everlasting attributes. As stewards of God and ambassadors for Christ, we are to center primarily on His administration and realize just how serious this teaching is to the overall maturity of the body of Christ today. This is not about religious gymnastics but about the vastness of kingdom dynamics.

Chapter IV
Understanding The Keys and Attributes of The Kingdom

Jesus said, "***And I will give you the keys of the kingdom of heaven, and whatever you bind on earth will be bound in heaven, and whatever you loose on earth will be loosed in heaven.***" Matthew 16:19. As a result of keys we were given, our goal, focus and desire should be to find out how, when and where to use His keys. Also, we are to find out what doors they open, isn't that true? The effects of our spoken words are spelled out as **nine** separate but interrelated keys in the Word of Truth. ***"Now, therefore, you are no longer strangers and foreigners, but fellow citizens with the saints and members of the household of God,***

20. having been built on the foundation of the apostles and prophets, Jesus Christ Himself being the chief cornerstone, 21. in whom the whole building, being fitted together, grows into a holy temple in the Lord, 22. in whom you also are being built together for a dwelling place of God in the Spirit." Ephesians 2:19-22.

Again beloved, please pay close attention to those seven underlined words in verses 19 to 22. It reveals that we are to see ourselves corporately **like a building which has nine floors**. Now, let us disclose what the real keys of the kingdom are and the great effects they are designed to produce. All of the nine (9) keys in The Scriptures are NOT spelled out as "KEYS" but as principles which requires our familiarity and choice on when and how to use them. "***It is the glory of God to conceal a thing: but the honor of kings is to search out a matter."*** Proverbs 25:2.

As it is clearly evident with natural things, when two elements are combined in their proper mix, they become highly potent and a more effective component. For example, the proper mix of hydrogen and oxygen; **H_2O** will become **water,** which is the most important and ubiquitous substance on earth. How about when we combine two independent poisons ie: **NaCL** Sodium and Chloride? You get **salt** which is in our body. What about a heterosexual male and a female who decides to get married, become intimate to have a **child(ren)**? This outcome is one of the most marvelous and astounding miracle of all! This is how YOU came into being; you are wonderfully made!

To further amplify the potent effect of combining ingredients, we are going to simplify them in a way which will ensure you become more familiar with them. Again, they involve our actions to implement God's provision which will yield advanced results. Also, this means, once they are implemented *–whether individually or combined–* they will open doors into the plethora of God's bounty. They are columns: A, B and C. Column **A** represents the **information**; Column **B** tells us the **action** and Column **C** will eventually yield the combined **results** on the next page. As a child of the Most High, there is...

A-----------------------**B** -------------------------- **C**

9. A **Culture** we must embrace which is____________________
8. A **Directive** we are to carry-out which is____________________
7. A **Commitment** we have to make which is__________________

6. **Discipline** we have to employ which include ________________
*5. **Humility** we have to exercise in order to be ________________
4. **Stewardship** we have to understand how __________________

3. **Words** we have to use which are ________________________
2. **Identity** we have to realize which is _______________________

1. Finally, there is **our foundation** which we have to protect which is:________ ______________.

Beloved, as you will notice, the information is listed in a descending order from 9- to -1 which can seem unusual. However, this was done intentionally. We deliberately did it this way to emphasize what is **first** or at the top like a building. Notice, there is the base or **foundation** which is of primary importance. No matter how high any structure ascends, the most important aspect is its base. It is no different with the things pertaining to the Kingdom of God.

Every structure built for longevity always hinges on its foundation. This is why extensive prior research is usually conducted for months or years to ensure it is able to withstand the immense weight. There are **eight** components which makes up the **kingdom of God** which are among us but only **one** foundation upon which they all stand. Now, we will unveil the total package delivered to you. In essence, as **stewards** of God and **ambassadors** for Christ, all the keys and their features are now spelled out in plain sight as follows: There is:

A	**B**	**C**
Information-------------------	**Action**--------------------------	**Results**

9. A **Culture** we must **embrace** which is-------------→ forgive & love
8. A **Directive** we are to **carry-out**: ie:Kingdom of God & rightn'ss
7. A **Commitment** we have to **make** which is worship & meditation

6. **Discipline** we have to **employ** which are prayer & fasting
*5. **Humility** we have to **exercise** in order to be----→ exalted by God
4. **Stewardship** we have to **understand** how finances $$ work

3. **Words** we have to **use** ie: **keys** are b/l, b/c, d/l, eiw, j/c (Pg #42)
2. **Identity** we have to **realize** which is----------→ who we are in Christ
1. Our foundation is Christ but our personal foundation is our thought **life.** This is what we must vigorously **protect** and take control of; we protect this foundation because it is our **most valuable asset to God.** Remember, these are essential elements.

Number three (#3) above, is the verse which Jesus unveiled about keys by stating, "***And I will give you the keys of the kingdom of heaven, and whatever you bind on earth will be bound in heaven, and whatever you loose on earth will be loosed in heaven***." Matthew 16:19. The two underlined words used by Matthew are defined as follows:

The word **bind** means to lock-up and secure.
The word **loose** means to allow or permit.

Now let us carefully reexamine the most important of the nine keys which is the foundation. As we all know, there are three perspectives which all assets take-on and encompass. They can be personal, business and/or real estate. Beloved, we are about to categorize the entire building structure in groupings of threes.

The top three (#'**9**, **8** and **7**) are **Godly directives**. "***For we are his workmanship, created in Christ Jesus unto good works***..." Eph. 2:10. And, at its summit, we know God's Word clearly says faith works by **love**. Therefore, we must embrace a holy and righteous lifestyle. "***Because it is written, be holy, for I am holy***." 1 Peter 1:16. Question; how does prosperity, blessings, profit and success come about in a believer's life? They **only** come about through **meditation** (#7) which is in the top three categories. Please turn to **Psalms 1:1-3, Psalms 19:14, Joshua 1:8** and **I Timothy 4:15.**

The next level is (#'**6**, **5** and **4**) which are **internal choices.** They are the ones which we personally control or they will govern us!

Finally, listed as (#**3**', **2** and **1**) are **results/outcomes** which we use every time our eyes are open. All three can work independently; however, they are more impactful together. Beloved, these are the nine (9) key components in God's Word which access, open and provide critical treasures in/for every believer's life! Also, let us bring to light all which we abbreviated in **#3** and spell them out for clarity; this way, we can all be on the same page of understanding along with knowing what our spoken words control.

They are:

B/C is blessings and cursing ----------------------------------James 3:10
B/L is bind and lose --------------------------------------Matthew 16:19
D/L is death and life -------------------------------------Proverbs 18:21
EIW is "every idle word" --------------------------------Matthew 12:36
J/C is justified or condemned----------------------------Matthew 12:37

Beloved, are we really grasping what the Word of God is clearly disclosing to us? Most new believers will love whereas, others will look to pick and find fault without accepting God's truth. Others will choose to return to their sandy foundation which they have built over time. Again, we should be taking what is written seriously enough to desire to change right away! Spoken words are one of our most powerful tools on earth. This is because words are disclosures of reality. Did you read, all unproductive words we use, we will stand trial for them? "***But I say unto you, that every idle word that men shall speak, they shall give account thereof in the Day of Judgment."*** Matthew 12:36. This is why Jesus gave us authority to control our circumstance through the use of faith filled spoken words. However, we must use His mighty name.

Why are we to use Jesus' name in all that we do? Because, "…***God also has highly exalted Him and given Him the name which is <u>above every name</u>, that at the name of Jesus <u>every knee should bow</u>, of those in heaven, and of those on earth, and of those under the earth, And that <u>every tongue should confess</u> that Jesus Christ is Lord, to the glory of God the Father***." Philippians 2:9-11. This license to use His matchless name gives us delegated authority in the spirit realm over circumstance, the devil/demons, sickness and disease.

However, as vital as all the terms associated with the keys are listed above, there is one-of-the-nine which sits right in the center *–like our heart–* of our body and relationship with God; that is #5: it is **<u>humility</u>**. When we choose to humble ourselves, The Word of Life says, "***And whoever exalts himself will be humbled, and he who humbles himself will be exalted***." Matthew 23:12. Who would not love to be exalted by God Himself? All of the nine keys *–above-* are accomplished in only one vessel which we know as our physical body.

Let us ask you a very appropriate question, **"<u>What do you claim to own that does not belong to you</u>**?" According to the Word of God, this would be your body! "***Or do you not know that your body is the temple of the Holy Spirit who is in you, whom you have from God, and you are <u>not your own</u>? For you were bought at a price; therefore, glorify God in your body and in your <u>spirit</u>, which are <u>God's</u>***." 1 Corinthians 6:19-20. A change in ownership or exchange occurs each time someone confess Jesus as **owner**!

Recognizing Our Highest Titles in God

As an heir of God, what is about to unfold is revolutionary, concise and true. Throughout God's Word, He assigned, called and attached various titles to His Offspring based on the situation. Just as keys are made to fit/open different locks, so too does our various titles fit different areas. God's intent was to let us realize who we are once we have become identified with Him through the new birth.

There is another sequence of nine (9) titles which are categorized in series of threes like the keys and attributes we mentioned earlier. They also fit and apply to believers in different situations and circumstances. God is interested in those who are more interested in Him! God has brilliantly done so to first provide **identity**; then, He spells out our **assignment** and finally what our ultimate **office** will be in the New Jerusalem. This is so that we begin to embrace things which provide eternal rewards. God did so in the hope that we **stop** seeking and focusing on money for temporary answers but first pursue His administration for solutions and eternal rewards.

These awesome and eternal titles appointed to us are as follows:

1..**Ambassadors** for Christ II Corinthians 5:20
2..**Stewards** Luke 16:1-3-------→1,2 & 3 are our **identity** right now!
3..**Ministers** II Corinthians 6:4

4..**Fishers of men:** Matt. 4:19
5..**Wise:** Prov. 11:30---------→ 4,5 & 6 are our earthly **assignments**!
6..**Light of the world** Matthew 5:16

7..**Judges:** 1Corinthians 6:3
8..**Kings**----------→ 7, 8, & 9; eventually, our New Jerusalem **office!**
9..**Priests:** Revelation 1:6

Again, ***"Do you not know that we shall judge angels? How much more, things that pertain to this life***?" I Corinthians 6:3. Today, it is rare that these titles are addressed, taught or spelled out to our young people. Some of us will judge the world, angels and things of this world! One Sunday morning when I was teaching in Pineville N.C about our identity, I asked the following question to the congregation. What if you were called downtown to the courthouse on Monday morning to **judge** every case placed before you; how would you feel? Someone softly expressed, "**unprepared**!" As you know, the Word of Truth did not make an error when it said, "***Study to show thyself approved unto God, a workman that needs not to be ashamed, rightly dividing the word of truth***." II Timothy 2:15. As ministers of God, we have got to examine where we are today and find out if we are constantly increasing in knowledge. Then, if we are called home tomorrow, did we fulfill our Godly assignment?

Understanding The Origin of God & Time

As a Youth Pastor/teacher who explains the Word of God to grade school students, I have found them to be curious yet receptive. I guess this is why Jesus only related His Kingdom to young people and not adults. "***Assuredly, I say to you, whoever does not receive the kingdom of God as a little child will by no means enter it***." Mark 10:15. The reason is, they are inquisitive, filled with excitement and are like sponges who absorb new information. Adults on the other hand, feel they have arrived and find it difficult to humble themselves and tend to reject something new because they have acquired a degree(s) of knowledge. Youths are not afraid to ask questions like; how, where and why? I beam with excitement and disclose what is spiritually correct and ask them questions.

One major combination question I cover with young people is, "**where did God come from; and, what is the origin of God**?" I start out by explaining to them what the word **eternal** means. I define it for them as, "<u>without beginning and without end</u>" which details God Himself! Also, I give them a great acronym for '**GOD**' which is **<u>G</u>**enius **<u>o</u>**f **<u>D</u>**esign. Then, I proceed to make the following statement; '**<u>before there was a beginning, there was God</u>**.' Therefore, God did NOT begin when Genesis began; God was before Genesis and the beginning." This conveys His origin. You see beloved, God has always existed but outside of how we measure time in years and millennia. The Scripture confirms, "***For a thousand years in Your***

sight are but as yesterday when it is past, and as a watch in the night. " Psalms 90:4. What we distinguish as thousands of years, God sees it as a millisecond. This is why there seems to be mass confusion as to the earth being millions/billions of years old. In the book of Revelation 10:6 it says when the angel flew by he said "...***there should be time no longer.***" This further confirms that we must be living in-time but there will come a period where there is no time measured; this is outside our timeframe. You see saint, time was not being recorded until God created the worlds/earth and man within a seven-day period and placed them *–male and female–* in The Garden of Eden. We know The Word of Life speaks of **God** the Father, **Jesus** Christ the Son and the awesome **Holy Spirit** of Truth. Man refers to this awesome union as ~~trinity~~. However, God points-out and only uses the correct combination in His Word as **"Godhead"** which is only written three (3) times. Acts 17:29, Romans 1:20 and Colossians 2:9.

The following is how I explain the **Godhead** to our young people; it is **NOT**, one plus one plus one (1+1+1) which equals 3; Instead, the **Godhead** is better understood as a multiple: (**1x1x1**) which equals (**=1**) and makes this union a potent co-equal entity. Entity, according to the Miriam-Webster's Dictionary, comes pretty close in describing the (**1x1x1**) combination as, 'something that has separate and distinct existence and objective or conceptual reality.' The Scripture defines this 'conceptual reality' as, ***"...The LORD our God is one LORD.***" Deuteronomy 6:4. Therefore, when ministering to others, we ought to use Godhead which is a mystery *–hidden truth–* that is undeniable, clearly stated and insightful.'

Now, the way I describe God and time to students is by using my cell phone. I hold it up and let them know the phone, a rectangle *–from one long side to the other–* represents time allotted for all mankind. Within the 6X3 rectangular boundaries is our lifespan which can average anywhere between sixty to ninety years. Outside that 2-3 inch screen represents eternity where time is **not** being tracked which is where God lives. It is through His Son we are able to enjoy natural life today and eternal life tomorrow which is outside of the rectangular timeline. God is the **One** who is indeed Great and Marvelous!

Not Servants, but Serving Our Gifts

As believers in Christ Jesus, one of our mission on earth is to first identify and know who we are; we are sons of God. See I John 3:1. This is why finding out who we are *–early in life–* in God is so critical. We impact others without even realizing it through our lifestyle. ***"Henceforth I call you not servants; for the servant knows not what his lord does; but I have called you friends..."*** John 15:15. ***"And because you are sons, God hath sent forth the Spirit of his Son into your hearts, crying, Abba, Father."*** Galatians 4:6. Please refer to the 'heart' diagram on page #8.

Also, God spells out the primary reason His own offspring perish and are destroyed; it is **not** because of the devil or people who do not like them. Destruction comes about primarily due to the absence of knowledge; God's Word confirms it this way, "***My people perish for lack of knowledge***." Hosea 4:6. As born again believers, we are sealed by His Holy Spirit ***–Ephesians 1:13–*** and are given keys ***–Matt. 16:19–*** to operate in earth's territory which makes us responsible for most things that occur. Therefore, we will be held accountable for duties assigned to us as stewards which we could have changed.

We are all aware that the highest earthly office in the United States is called the president who is also a **public servant**. However, this does not make our president a servant; it simply means he is to **serve his office**, not as a servant or slave to anyone. In-fact, a public servant is to attend to the citizen's needs; not the other way around. Just as presidents or prime ministers/leaders serve the people, we are to carry-out our responsibility to serve and humble ourselves toward others.

"We then that are strong ought to bear the infirmities of the weak, and not to please ourselves." Romans 15:1. As a child of The Most High who are given keys, it makes it imperative that we become very familiar with keys and find out what locks/doors they open in this life as well as what level of access they provide. No one gives keys to strangers or servants but only to those who are in authority and a "**need to know/have**" basis; isn't that true? As citizens, we choose when to use them and where. Also, as His offspring with responsibilities, it means at some point we will have to give an account of how, when and what we used them to release or lock-up; isn't that true as well?

One question we should **definitely** want to provide an answer to God for is, "**what have you done with the keys which I gave you**?" Again, keys open, (un)locks, secures and access situations including important and private information. And, as 'Ambassadors for Christ', we represent God on earth just as ambassadors represent one country to another. Remember, this is who we really are! We represent Heaven to earth! God's Holy Spirit instructed the writers to call His offspring 'ambassadors for Christ to serve their gift. "***Most assuredly, I say to you, he who believes in Me, the works that I do he will do also; and greater works than these he will do, because I go to My Fathe***r." John 14:12.

Did Jesus call us light of the world, heirs of God, salt of the earth, faithful and righteous? Yes! Again, we no longer called servants! The widely taken out of context verse, "well done good and faithful servants" **Matt. 25:23** pertains to those who are in-tune with God, knows who they are and ardently desire to carry out all their assignments as stewards. If we are not doing so, we are not being faithful stewards. Jesus was *–and is–* King who served all mankind and provided for others but never called Himself a servant. However, He is more appropriately called the **Servant-King**! Jesus said, "…***I have come that they may have life, and that they may have it more abundantly***." John 10:10. This means Jesus came to reveal to citizens who they are, become aware of their capabilities and to be their living example.

Our young people get it right away and desire to step-up their game. They embrace what God's Library says about them and are excited that all things are possible for them if they dare to believe God's Word. This is why I provide detailed Scripture to further encourage them to memorize and always apply God's Principles to their situation. I do so by suggesting that they read a corresponding Proverb *–in the Old Treaty–* to the day of the week. This way, they learn Godly principles every day, month and year.

Jesus Said…

"And I appoint unto you a kingdom, as my Father has appointed unto me." Luke 22:29. The underlined root word, **appoint** means to **bestow** and **confer**. In other words, Jesus was saying, my Father bestowed something on me; now that I am departing, I am assigning that same responsibility on you. This also means it is up to the recipient to announce the right message of The Kingdom wherever they go. Jesus confirmed; "a***nd as you go, preach,*** –announce– ***saying, 'The kingdom of heaven is at hand.***" Matthew 10:7.

Jesus did not say to proclaim His life, the cross, faith or water baptism. He was giving specific instruction on what to proclaim to the world. Do you remember when Jesus was before Pilate, again He clarified by stating, "***My Kingdom is not of this world***…" John 18:36; He did not say, it was NOT in the world.

This is critical to point out early in our understanding of His Word because Jesus brought an entire governmental administration to earth that is both present and invisible. We will read what the Prophet Isaiah mentioned shortly. In March of 2016, I was teaching a class of young teens about Jesus' deity and relationship to His Father. After the session, they were all called into the sanctuary. One of the main speakers asked all the teen, "what did you learn from Minister Paul's teaching?

There was an aura of silence for a few moments. One student who was as bold as a lion, raised his hand and said, I learned who Jesus is; the minister asked, who is He? The student responded with the most profound and stunningly accurate summary concerning Jesus; he said, "**Jesus is the visible image of the invisible God**." See Colossians 1:15. The sanctuary was in awe, surprised and excited as I was! Our young people are carrying out the message of Jesus and they know who He is and the message they are to convey.

As saints of God, what message or information comes to mind upon reading the above verse? Has God really bestowed a kingdom's responsibility on you? Yes, He has! And, does it mean we have received something that we will eventually be asked to give an account? Or, was Jesus simply making a statement without any significance and responsibility? Blessed of the Lord, rest assured we will all have to give an account of what was delivered to us as His stewards. Also, based on Scriptural evidence, I am convinced about two profound questions which all believers will be asked of God; they are:

First, '**give an account of your stewardship**!' This means we are **not** owners of anything we think we possess because everything is on loan to us from God and we become accountable! Furthermore, all we "think we own" is for distribution to others so everyone is raised to the same plateau of wealth which is called **commonwealth**. "***Now the multitude of those who believed were of one heart and one soul; neither did anyone say that any of the things he possessed was his own, but they had all things in common***." Acts 4:32.

This type of mind-set is not prevalent today and seems to be deleted from our hard-drive. The second question is even more astounding because it requires us to **use** something we were given. In other words, we will have access and some degree of control.

The second stunning follow-up question which we will ALL be asked is, '**what have you done with the keys I gave you**?' As a born again believer in Christ, we were all given keys! Therefore, it would be wise and in our best interest to become very familiar with what we were given; wouldn't you agree? As offspring, the kingdom and its keys are critical components which we are to seek passionately and understand thoroughly.

The primary reason is the accountability factor! "***till we all come in the unity of the faith, and of the knowledge of the Son of God, unto a perfect man, unto the measure of the stature of the fullness of Christ***." Ephesians 4:13. Jesus knew that if we were given keys, at some point we should ask Him, what are they for? And, what do they open-up or, lock-out? I think most of us would regard this as accurate!

Chapter V
Jesus' Priority For All Stewards

As you know, most people become uneasy when they are asked anything Biblical/religious because no one likes to feel they are being 'put-on-the-spot or tested whether they know the details or not. Over the years, I have found two questions which produce this type of uneasiness. They are:

What does The Word say answers all things in the **Old** Testament?
What does The Word say answers all things in the **New** Treaty?

Most people and some pastors/ministers who are money conscious usually default to **Ecclesiastics 10:19** which says, "...***money answers all things***." This answer appeals to just about anyone in leadership positions especially those who teach a prosperity Gospel. And, this approach appeals to money seekers as their primarily focus on the multiple streams of income process. Even those without the knowledge of God would vie for this Scripture because they feel they can always use more to improve or better their situation.

However, the answer to the second question is not popular and is only unveiled to the ardent seekers of God's Word. Jesus clearly outlined what answers all things in the New Testament. He said, "...*seek **FIRST the Kingdom of God and His righteousness and all these things shall be added unto you***." Matthew 6:33. Luke's account of the same subject is as follows: "***But seek the kingdom of God, and all these things shall be added to you***." Luke 12:31. Both Matthew and Luke's message are identical.

These statements detail Jesus' priority which lets us know what our pursuit should be above everything else; they both rank this above food, shelter, clothing and things we desire. As offspring, God wants to redirect our focus from the natural earthly things to pursue the treasures concealed in His kingdom. Remember, "***It is the glory of God to conceal a thing: but the honor of kings is to search out a matter***." Proverbs 25:2.

How about this? **There is one thing you should seek which will provide you with everything you need!** The answer Jesus provided above is both our primary directive and a stunningly accurate answer. Also, it is the only treasure God provided for all mankind especially His stewards who have become ambassadors for Christ. The reason we are so repetitive and direct about our relationship status, is that most people live life the way they want, then call on God for help as adverse situations arise in their life.

My former mother-in law gave me one of the most stunningly accurate phrase about "Christians." She said, "*people are people first, then they are Christians*." Precise, profound and I found it to be the obvious reality in life today who ever I meet. Everyone does what they want to do first, then hold to their identification with Christ second. Do you remember when God showed Isaiah what The Messiah was bringing to earth? It was to present the solution to man's problem including the financial sector of their lives.

This great-find was directed to everyone. And, it was not some ordinary administration but a process designed to leave the greatest imprint on the entire world's population forever. Now we are about to face some other startling truths so that we find both clarity and answers in the Word of God. It is critical to point out that the entire ~~Bible~~ "**Word of Truth**" is **not** all about the kingdom of God! As we stated earlier, the Kingdom dynamics was brought and delivered to earth by Jesus which was what Isaiah told us. "…***of the increase of His government and peace there will be no end***..." Isaiah 9:7. Let us ask; what was Joseph of Arimathaea waiting for? See Mark 15:43.

Jesus' priorities for those who are identified with Him was and still is to pursue, seek and know about the administration which He brought. Remember, Paul said that the Holy Spirit will be "…***distributing to each one individually as He wills."*** I Corinthians 12:11. And, since this is true, then our new goal and emphasis should be about The Distributor. "***For as many as are led by the "Spirit of God," they are the sons of God***. "Romans 8:14. As we humble ourselves and choose to be led by Him, He can become the driver, teacher and revealer of concealed things in our midst.

Jesus' Two Forty-Day Periods & Paul's Two and One-Half Years of Ministry

Beloved, it is spelled out in God's Word that there are two major forty-day time-lines during Jesus' ministry. "***And He was there in the wilderness for forty days, tempted by satan, and was with the wild beasts. And the angels ministered to Him.***" Mark 1:13. As the Scripture stated, this was the first important forty-day period and testing of Jesus' ministry. During this time, He was strengthened spiritually but physically His body desperately craved sustenance.

The other significant phase was after His resurrection. "..***To whom He also presented Himself alive after His suffering by many infallible proofs, being seen by them during forty days and speaking of the things pertaining to the kingdom of God.***" Acts 1:3. First, it was to provide proof of His resurrection. What else was Jesus doing throughout this other significant interval? What was He teaching or revealing? There must have been another valid reason and extremely urgent message which He needed to reaffirm or substantiate, wouldn't you agree? How about the following considerations?

1--Maybe, after three and a half (3 ½) years, the disciples still did not comprehend the magnitude of His administration.
2—How about, their focus was still not where it should be.
3--Maybe, Jesus knew they would still have to hear it for almost six weeks in order to really get it!
4--Finally, the time was to provide evidence of His resurrection.

God's government is so vast and immeasurable that Jesus spent three and a half years teaching it using metaphors, similes, examples and almost every common object of His day to convey this message. As you know, He used a net, keys, pearl, like a man traveling, the pearl of great price, mustard seed, leaven and a host of other examples. We need to redirect our attention and find out more of its significance.

Also, did you know that the Apostle Paul preached the message of the kingdom of God for ninety days straight as well as two consecutive years? First, "***And he went into the synagogue, and spake boldly for the space of three months, disputing and persuading the things concerning the kingdom of God***." Acts 19:8. We need to ask ourselves, why only this message for such an extended period? How about this rarely mentioned find? Paul proclaimed the kingdom message both at the beginning and the end of his ministry. Let's prove it with Scripture! Have you ever heard one topic being taught for over two years? "***And when they had appointed him a day, there came many to him into his lodging; to whom he expounded and testified the kingdom of God.***" Acts 28:23.

30 "And Paul dwelt two whole years in his own hired house, and received all that came in unto him, 31 preaching the kingdom of God, and teaching those things which concern the Lord Jesus Christ, with all confidence, no man forbidding him." Acts 28:30-31. You see beloved, what we are hearing on Saturdays, Sundays and Wednesday night Bible Study are not the real message which Jesus, Paul and the Apostles taught. The real emphasis should be familiarizing saints with the *–administration–* Kingdom of God. Only this message will prepare us to rule and reign with Christ in the New Jerusalem as kings, priests and judges. See page 44, #'s 7--9.

The Titles, Details & Roles of The Holy Spirit

There are two particular words we are about to combine and ascribe to God's awesome Holy Spirit. The title and words are "**GOD'S** and **PEACE**" which according to Jesus, **peace** is what He brings. "***Peace I leave with you, My peace I give to you; not as the world gives do I give to you. Let not your heart be troubled, neither let it be afraid***." John 14:27.

The first word is "**God's.**" In businesses today, titles represent status, positions and they reveal just how important a person is to an organization. We did this so that believers can easily relate the Holy Spirit's specific roles, functions and various responsibilities. Again, these two dynamic words we are about to unveil as acronyms are '**God's**' and the second word is '**Peace.**' This way we can become more familiar with His character, position and relevance to offices we recognize today. The person of the Holy Spirit can be identified with:

G-overnor
O-verseer
D-irector
S-upervisor

P-rincipal
E-xecutive
A-dministrator
C-EO, CFO, COO
E-xecutive Director

These designations cover some of what God's Holy Spirit does and who He is like in today's world. Also, there is another word which we will assign to Him; it too is spelled out in another acronym called, **GREAT**. This word vividly defines some of His marvelous attributes in believer's lives which we will be mentioning several times throughout the book. And, we are to take these five vitamins every day. They are easy to swallow, digest and apply in our daily devotional time with the Lord. As we choose to acknowledge Him, He will:

G uide us into **all** truth-- John 16:13
R emind us of **all** things-------------------------------------- John 14:26
E mpower us to act on earth on Heaven's behalf ------------ Acts 1:8
A bide in us because we are God's temple on earth-------- I Cor. 6:18
T each us **all** things as ambassadors for Christ------------- John 14:26

Each believer who chooses to envelop an ambassador's mindset and carry out their stewardship assignment will be able to provide the right answers to those in need. Again, the Scripture says, ***"Study to shew thyself approved unto God, a workman that needeth not to be ashamed, rightly dividing the word of truth."*** II Timothy 2:15.

We provided these Scriptures in order for the reader to become more closely knit with what the Holy Spirit can do for them every day, if they acknowledge Him. Jesus said, ***"But the Helper, the Holy Spirit, whom the Father will send in My name, He will teach you all things, and bring to your remembrance all things that I said to you."*** John 14:16, 26, John 15:26-27 and John 16:13.

Furthermore, the Word of Life states, "***For as many as are led by the Spirit of God, they are the sons of God.***" Romans 8:14, Galatians 3:26, 4:6 and John 1:12. There is a lost and dying world out there that needs the right information and proper guidance. Only when we choose to be led by the Spirit of Christ, then He will reveal to us when, where, who and what to say to someone as He did to the apostles.

Today, our most important pursuit is money, entertainment, music, medication, and sports when we should be spending quality time to get to know the Spirit of God; He desires relationship and communion as does The Father. We are to memorize the following **A–to–Z** about Him which shows just how awesome and diverse He is along with his versatility among citizens in His kingdom. In doing so, we are reminding ourselves of who He is and His involvement in our life. God's REMARKABLE Spirit of Truth will prepare citizens to "…***be ready always to give an answer to every man that asks you a reason of the hope that is in you with meekness and fear."*** I Peter 3:15.

We provided some valuable information and neatly packaged it just for you! And, it is for immediate use upon receiving it to your address; so please accept and open the package below. All it requires is that you meditate on what God's Holy Spirit does from **A** to **Z.** The time you spend is never time wasted, but time invested. **He**:

Abides in me, and --John 14:16
Bring all things to my remembrance, He, ------------------John 14:26
Comforts me, He--John 14:16
Discloses the future unto me, He ------------------------------John 16:13
Empowers me, He is the --- Acts 1:8
Fire of God in me; He --------------------------- Luke 3:16, Acts 19:1-6
Glorifies the Lord Jesus, He is my ----------------------------John 16:14

Helper, my -- John 14:26
Instructor, who---Acts 13:2
Justifies me, He-- I Corinthians 6:11
Knows all things; I am-- John 14:26
Led by Him; He is the -------------------------------------- Romans 8:14
Meek and quiet Spirit; He is -------------------------------------I Peter 3:4
Not about word, but Power; He is my -----------------------I[t] Cor. 4:20

Ointment poured out; He is the-------------------- Joel 2:28, Acts 2:17
Power & the Peace of God; He has all the------------------- John 14:27
Qualities of the Godhead, He is the------------------------ Romans 1:20
Revealer of <u>truth</u> and <u>secrets</u>, He has------------------------- Luke 2:26
Sealed me and He speak to me, He ---------Ephesians 1:13, Acts 13:2
Teaches and Transports me, He is --------------John 14:26, Acts 8:39
Unique and Unlimited, He is------------------------------ Matthew 19:26

Vast and Vivacious, He is -------------------------------- Matthew 28:18
Wonderful and worth pursuing, He is my **---------------**Matthew 6:33
X = NEWS, North East West and South and I --------------John16:13
Yield to Him; He is the ------------------------------------- Romans 6:16
Zeal of The Lord---Isaiah 9:7

Always remember, He heads-up the kingdom of God on earth. Therefore, by meditating on your newly arrived **ABC-Z** package, you will be establishing a better relationship with the Holy Spirit; He will G.R.E.A.T you in both the things of God as well as in dealing with the day-to-day activities and people. See **Proverbs 3:5-6.**

"***But you shall receive power when the Holy Spirit has come upon you...***" Acts 1:8. Also, "***in humility correcting those who are in opposition, if God perhaps will grant them repentance, so that they may know the truth.***" II Tim. 2:25. In doing so, we are able to provide others with accurate answers to their situation and problems.

The Gifts/Administrations of The Holy Spirit

God's gifts to His offspring are as follows; "***For to one is given the word of <u>wisdom</u> through the Spirit, to another the word of***

***knowledge* through the same Spirit, to another *faith* by the same Spirit, to another gifts of *healings* by the same Spirit, to another the working of *miracles*, to another *prophecy*, to another *discerning* of spirits, to another *different* kinds of tongues, to another the *interpretation* of tongues**." 1 Corinthians 12:8-10.

Now, we are going to categorize these nine (9) gifts in a slightly different arrangement than is stated above. My sincere intent is to form a clearer picture in our transformed mind so that they will be better understood collectively in categories of three. The Apostle Paul began **NOT** with wisdom but with **Word** of wisdom; then, he mentioned **Word** of knowledge. Both these terms are only mentioned once in this order throughout God's Word.

1..**Word of wisdom**	
2..**Word of knowledge**-----------------→	1,2 & 3 are **Revelation** Gifts
3..**Discernment of Spirits**	
4.. **Faith**	
5..**Gifts of Healing**--------------------------→	4,5 & 6 are **Power** Gifts
6..**Working of Miracles**	
7..**Prophecy**	
8..**Divers kinds of tongues**------------------→	7, 8, & 9 are **Vocal** Gifts
9..**Interpretation of tongues**	

It is rare that these gifts are categorized in Bible Schools, Seminaries or even among mature citizens in the body of Christ. When I speak to some believers, they feel they have one in particular which is listed as **(#3) discernment**. Many people confuse their own human perceptive abilities with that of "**discernment of spirits**" which is only given by the Holy Spirit for specific purposes and for certain times.

It is only in particular instances where the Holy Spirit will provide insight which will allow you to call-out/identify a particular spirit or in specific areas. For example, "***And it came to pass, as we went to prayer, a certain damsel possessed with a spirit of divination met us, which brought her masters much gain by soothsaying:***

The same followed Paul and us, and cried, saying, these men are the servants of the Most-High God, which shew unto us the way of salvation. 18. And this did she many days. But Paul, being grieved, turned and said to the spirit, I command thee in the name of Jesus Christ to come out of her. And he came out the same hour." Acts 16:16-18. This is what it is like when we are engaged in doing The Lord's work. Only then will He enlighten, expose and reveal what is not of God and what is; this way, we can do something about it!

All citizens are to live a pure lifestyle before God and man every day! The kingdom is God's work; whereas, the gospel is our assignment to understand, proclaim, pursue. As friends of God, if we choose to spend quality time with the Holy Spirit during our devotional time of study, He will provide the appropriate gift necessary to address what you will be facing but at the right time. This is so that God alone gets the glory; not us! "…***I will not let my reputation be tarnished, and I will not share my glory with idols***!" Isaiah 48:11. This means with anyone or anything!

All of the nine gifts which the Holy Spirit can distribute are designed to prepare us for leadership in the ultimate *–third–* kingdom which we detailed on pages 11-14. And, at the present time, Jesus is preparing to bring the New Jerusalem to earth very soon. All of the information is insightful and marvelous as well as provide a detailed synopsis of His kingdom. Earlier we stated, the Gospel –**Good News**– is NOT about Jesus' death, burial and resurrection, it's about The Awesome Kingdom of God.

Even though it is indeed Good News that Jesus gave His life so that all of mankind can come back to God, this is NOT the Gospel. One relevant and pertinent fact to consider about the perceived gospel being: the **death**, **burial** and **resurrection**," it was never made public by Jesus; neither did John the Baptist proclaim it at any time during his ministry. As you have read, each time Jesus' death, burial and resurrection was mentioned it was **NEVER** understood by the people or anyone prior to His temporary death! Finally, in Luke 7:22, it clearly spells out that you do not preach someone's death, burial and resurrection to poor people but "Good News" of a new administration they can access to change their life and circumstance. This is good news!

Understanding The Purpose for Both Treaties

Beloved, we are about to provide two dynamic words in the columns below which will define the significance of both the Old and New Testament. These words which stands vertically details what their main purpose were and what they represent. Each one hinges on the other without minimizing the other. They are:

The Old Testament was about:	**The New Testament** is about:
H-istory ----------------------------	**P**-ower & fulfillment of prophecy
O-rdinance-------------------------	**O**-utpouring of the Spirit of God
P-rophecy --------------------------	**W**-itness(es) of Jesus & Wisdom
E-xamples -------------------------	**E**-ternal life & entrance by birth
--	**R**-edemption & Rights

We know the Scripture clearly states, "***all** scripture is given by inspiration of God, and is profitable for doctrine, for reproof, for correction, for instruction in righteousness*." II Timothy 3:16. However, in order to pin-point and further understand the purpose for both the Old and the New Testament, let us turn to a very familiar encounter. The Scripture which we are to delve into is the most profound of all teaching which details Jesus' status and superiority above everyone else.

We are referring to what took place between Jesus, Peter, James and John along with Moses and Elijah on a high mountain. This was recorded in both the book of Matthew and Luke. Some ministers and books refer to this conference as '**The Mount of Transfiguration**' experience in Matthew 17:1-9.

Whenever I teach this lesson, I start out by asking a very interesting but thought provoking question; I ask, please summarize what took place on that mountain between Jesus, Moses and Elijah using just one-word? The answers and responses ranged from no response, to an illustration, to showing Jesus' brilliance, a change in glory or it was about Jesus' uniqueness. I submit to you, the most profound insight about this significant God-ordained gathering was about "**transference**." Let us dissect this teaching *–not story–* so that we can obtain the right answers and gain proper understanding. Jesus' unveiling was not about His countenance brightened as never before seen or experienced.

Even Moses *–when he was alive physically thousands of years earlier–* prophesied about The Messiah Jesus by stating, "***The LORD your God will raise up for you a Prophet like me from your midst, from your brethren. Him you shall hear.***" Deuteronomy 18:15. Again, this only referenced Jesus and transference because of superiority! Now, Moses was seeing this prophecy being fulfilled in plain sight thousands of years later.

Again, this entire meeting was primarily about transference from the Old Covenant standards to the New Administration's supremacy for those born-again in Christ. These are also offspring who "***have been made the righteousness of God in Him***" *–II Cor. 5:21–* and **sealed** by His Holy Spirit. *Ephesians 1:13*. There are some who think that the Old Treaty is still the standard to live–by which is not accurate.

Jesus said, ***"Did not Moses give you the law, yet none of you keeps the law…***?" John 7:19. Also, the Word of Truth says, "***But now hath He** –Jesus– **obtained a more excellent ministry, by how much also He is the mediator of a better covenant, which was established upon better promises."*** Hebrews 8:6.

Finally, Jesus said "***I have come that they may have life, and that they may have it more abundantly***." John 10:10. Please review previous page and then take a very close look at the upcoming page. In others words, review pages sixty and sixty-two comparatively.

Difference/Purpose of The Old & New Treaty

As diligent seekers of truth and answers, when we carefully examine both the Old and New treaties side-by-side, we see a much more vivid picture. However, Jesus said, "***Till heaven and earth pass, one jot or one tittle shall in no wise pass from the law, till all be fulfilled***." Matthew 5:18. We are to remember its history, ordinances, principles and examples. Also, we are still to respect, become familiar and refer to the Old as long as it does not conflict with Jesus' teachings. On numerous occasions you have read where Jesus referred to The Old Treaty and said, "***you have heard it said...but I say***..." Now let's examine both characteristics as well as their vast differences below.

The Law: Old Treaty		Jesus: Grace / New Treaty
1-No armor		Access to the whole armor of God
2-No authority		Authority over demons & satan
3-Angels were called sons of God		Believers called sons of God
4-Cannot keep the Commandments		Love fulfills all Ten
5-Curse of the law		Redeemed from it
6-No eternal life		Everlasting life
7-Examples	--→	Excellence
8-Fear of death		No fear of death
9-No redeemer	**–JESUS–**	Redeemer of man
10-The dead went to Abraham's bosom		Present w/The Lord
11-Promises		Much better promises
12-No power		Both power & authority
13-No savior		Jesus is Savior of The World
14-No peace		We can access the Prince of Peace

As we know, there are multitudes of other promises left for us as stewards; this is just one reason we are called heirs. "***And if children, then heirs—heirs of God and joint heirs with Christ, if indeed we suffer with Him, that we may also be glorified together***." Romans 8:17. An heir is a person legally entitled to property or the belongings of another upon a particular person's death. We are the inheritors!

Also, the Word of Truth states, "***by which have been given to us exceedingly great and precious promises, that through these you may be partakers of the divine nature, having escaped the corruption that is in the world through lust.***' II Peter 1:4.

Remember when we mentioned the number one problem with humans is identity crisis, some people do not realize the superiority of the New Treaty to the Old because of Jesus. This is why we placed them side-by-side so that we can observe the vast difference between administrations. The illustration was designed to answer the identity crisis question. And, we can observe what was in place and what has taken place which is far better because of Jesus; the difference maker!

"Our Most Vital Component to God"

As you may be able to tell, I like to ask questions. One of which I ask fellow believers is, "**what is our most valuable and important asset to God**?" The answers vary widely from commitment to reading and studying His Word. The right response is our thought life which reigns supreme because this is where everything begins. And, its value to God is as critical as blood is to our physical body.

Do you remember when Jesus mentioned about a person's mind in relationship to God? Jesus said, "***These people draw near to Me with their mouth, and honor Me with their lips, But their heart*** –mind– ***is far from Me."*** Matthew 15:8. As citizens in God's kingdom, He is more interested in the condition of our minds or mental-state than He is about anything else. We are to begin shifting the focus towards guarding our minds so it does not veer off the right path and into the gutter of lustful thoughts and debauchery.

Hence the reason for meditating in His Word "…***day and night…***" Joshua 24:15. Anything we value, we are to vigorously protect, wouldn't you agree? God is always providing valuable information to His Offspring so that they stay on track. Why are we so insistent on the high importance of our thought life? This is because it is the least mentioned area preached on or taught and even less attention has been directed to its status and capabilities. Most true believers are not consciously aware that The Word of Truth says, "***The thought** of **foolishness is sin***..." Proverbs 24:9. What are we to do with foolish thoughts? Cast them away, get rid of them by asking God to forgive you. Opposing/lustful thoughts and imaginations require the same approach to God as if we sinned physically!

This is why the Word of Life states, "...***casting down imaginations and every high thing that exalts itself against the knowledge of God and bringing into captivity every thought to the obedience of Christ***." II Corinthians 10:5. God knew we would need a total restructuring of our thought life which we are fully in control of. God blesses us through meditating on His Word and our proper thought life and less of what we do. **Our thoughts reign supreme to God**!

"The Word of Truth" specifically confirms and lists them as follows:

1–As a man **thinks** in his subconscious mind, so is he......Prov. 23:7
2–God will keep us in **perfect peace** whose **mind**............Isaiah 26:3
3–**"We have the _____of Christ"**....................................I Cor. 2:16
4–Be transformed, how? By renewing it......................Romans 12:1-2
5–We bring into captivity every **thought**.............................II Cor. 10:5
6–We are to **think** on things that are true, honest...................Phil. 4:8
7–The Word of God is a discerner of our **thoughts**..........Hebr. 4:12
8–Again, the **thought** of foolishness is sin...... ....Prov. 24:9
9–Out of the abundance of the **mind**, the mouth.........Matthew 12:34

These eye-opening scriptures are only a few of many other specific verses which reveal to us just how critical our thoughts and minds are to God. Also, it exposes the great impact it has on our relationship with Him, His Son Jesus and His Spirit of Truth.

As sons of God, the proper mindset/attitude is vitally important in both the natural everyday development as well as in every aspect of our relationship with God. And, did you know His Word says, ***In the day when God shall judge the secrets of men by Jesus Christ according to my gospel***?" Romans 2:16. How revealing this is! Beloved, we are to change old mindset so that we can move into victory in Christ.

#1, Our Mind and Imagination

Beloved, our sensual thoughts will **ALWAYS** lead us down the road of desiring personal satisfaction if we allow it. Naturally, we all desire to fulfill extreme cravings which we know as debauchery or sensual pleasures. In my quest to find precise answers about ourselves, I arrived at the following; "sin is more about what we think and less about what we do." This is why Jesus told several people, "***Go and sin no more***." John 8:11. Sin is a choice; it's not something that falls in our laps.

The power is in all of us not to sin because it really comes down to our choice! In other words, we choose to sin because it is pleasurable. And, life is all about choices. Take a look at what God's Word says about Moses. "…***choosing rather to suffer affliction with the people of God, than to enjoy the pleasures of sin for a season***." Hebrews 11:25. We all know and realize that there is pleasure in sin. However, we are not to allow its tentacles to hold us in bondage.

As mature believers, some of us know it was first the imaginations of the thoughts of man that repulsed God; not their deeds. "***And GOD saw that the wickedness of man was great in the earth, and that every imagination of the thoughts of his heart was only evil continually***." Genesis 6:5. And, are we aware that one of the six things God hates is the thing we liked doing the most? One of the six is, "***A heart** –mind– **that devises wicked imaginations***..." Proverbs 6:18. Let us take another look at those two underlined words.

We know, as ambassadors for Christ, some things may be familiar for most of us reading this book; to others, it may be brand new. Let us bring to light that Jesus often times addressed the thoughts of people in a crowd and not what was apparent or physically in front of Him. "***And he said unto them, why are you troubled? and why do thoughts arise in your hearts***?" Luke 24:38. Again, please refer to the diagram concerning heart on page #8. Why would Jesus address the thoughts of man? It is because of the importance and the value it possesses; this is where the real questions lie! Again, let's see what is mentioned in the book of Proverbs regarding all men. "***For as he thinks in his***

heart*, so is he..."** Proverbs 23:7. Did you know thoughts precede prayer, worship, praise and anything else you can conceive? As offspring, we know it is those whose mind is stayed on God are the ones who will experience true peace on earth. The Word of Truth clarifies these remarkable statements, "You will keep him in perfect peace, whose mind is stayed on You, because he trusts in You***." Isaiah 26:3.

Also, how are we transformed? "***And do not be conformed to this world, but be transformed by the renewing of your mind, that you may prove what is that good and acceptable and perfect will of God***." Romans 12:2. In essence, only a transformed thinking will allow us to prove what is good; it will bring peace; it will reveal what is acceptable and it is complete according to God's standard.

As we mentioned earlier, there are multitudes of other Scriptures which addresses the potent nature of our thoughts, the foundation of sin and heights we can attain in God. This is by choosing to keep our thought life pure. Beloved, if we sin in thought we are to verbally confess it to The Lord just as we would any other transgression. The Scripture confirms. "...***the thought of foolishness is sin***..." Proverbs 24:9.

Chapter VI
<u>Clarity</u> on Jesus' Death, Burial and Resurrection

Throughout Jesus' ministry, He only proclaimed one message *–but touched on various topics–* for the entire three and one-half years. Beloved, contrary to popular sermons, Jesus did NOT teach about His death, suffering and being resurrected. This statement contradicts what most people have heard, believed and taught; As we previously and briefly mentioned, whenever He declared it, no one understood what He was talking about. "***Howbeit Jesus spake of his death: but they thought that he had spoken of taking of rest in sleep***." John 11:13.

Secondly, did you know that Jesus' own Disciples did not know and was even confused about His death and resurrection? Do you remember when Jesus told them He was going to be killed? Peter said, no so Lord. Then Jesus, "***...rebuked Peter, saying, "Get behind Me, Satan! For you are not mindful of the things of God, but the things of men***." Mark 8:33. In our modern phrase, Jesus was saying, 'get out of my face Peter, what you're saying is of the devil and you have no clue what you are saying!'

Next, when Jesus alluded to His death, it was <u>**not**</u> understood and was deliberately hidden from them. "***Jesus said unto them***, "***for the Son of man shall be delivered into the hands of men. But they understood not this saying, and it was hid from them, that they perceived it not: and they feared to ask him of that saying***." Luke 9:43-45. This statement was mentioned to fulfill prophecy, not for the media or public broadcasting.

On yet another occasion Jesus said, "***they will scourge Him –Jesus– and kill Him. And the third day He will rise again. <u>But they understood none of these things</u>; this saying was hidden from them, and they did not know the things which were spoken.***" Luke 18:34. Furthermore, when Jesus alluded to His death, it too was misunderstood by the hearers. Jesus said, "*...destroy this temple, and in three days I will raise it up*." John 2:19. The Jews grossly misconstrued this statement as well. "***Then said the Jews, Forty and six years was this temple in building, and wilt thou rear it up in three days***?" John 2:20. As you know, Jesus was referencing His body and the Jews associated it to the physical temple of worship in Jerusalem.

Now, let us address the specific section which mentions the sequence of Jesus' death, burial and resurrection in this order. On this particular occasion, Paul was defending a theological argument, he stated, "***For I delivered unto you first of all that which I also received, how that Christ died for our sins according to the scriptures, And that he was buried, and that he rose again the third day according to the scriptures..."*** 1 Corinthians 15:3-4.

As stewards, please receive what is about to be unveiled. The reason Paul made this statement was to defend a religious disagreement with the Jews because they missed the fact that The Messiah actually came already, suffered, died and was resurrected according to the Scriptures. This address of Jesus was done years after He went back to be with His Father and God. Beloved, God is all about disclosing correct information so that we are able to disseminate the same accurate information clearly, concisely and in unison to the world.

What is "The Key of Knowledge?"

The four words in quotes above, are only mentioned once throughout the Word of God in this particular format. Jesus clearly spelled-out exactly what 'the key of knowledge' was as well as its magnitude and impact it would have on those who enter its spiritual realm. Let us now share both Luke's account and Matthew's description which will merge and provide one clear understanding. Jesus said, "***woe to you lawyers! For you have taken away the key of knowledge. You did not ENTER in yourselves, and those who were entering in you hindered***." Luke 11:52.

In other words, Jesus was saying they have taken away something that was not theirs to take. And, did Jesus just reveal that we access this realm; **not** go to it? **Yes**! During the time of Jesus, when you '**woe**' someone, it meant to warn, caution and to bring to light an adverse action which was deliberate. Jesus' warning was directed to religious leaders who were doing what was contrary to what they were fully aware of. This is like you having water and knowing others are thirsty but refusing to give them drink to quench their thirst. Now let us look at Matthew's description who exploited the religious ruler's hypocrisy to an even higher level.

He recorded Jesus as saying, "***But woe to you, scribes and Pharisees, hypocrites! For you shut up the kingdom of heaven against men; for you neither go in yourselves, nor do you allow those who are entering to go in***." Matthew 23:13. Beloved, where Matthew mentioned the "**kingdom of Heaven,**" Luke wrote about this to be the "**key of knowledge**." Remember on pages 34 to 38 where it detailed why Matthew uses kingdom of Heaven and the kingdom of God interchangeably?

We also stated why the other writers only used kingdom of God to describe the same event. We now know Matthew's accounts and Luke's description are precise and accurate because God's awesome Holy Spirit is the key to either term. When we accurately define 'the key of knowledge,' **it is the governance of the Holy Spirit over the nine gifts which He personally distributes any or all of them to believers as situation warrants and as He sees fit.**

Paul confirms Him as being the distributor/supervisor of the gifts; "***But one and the same Spirit works all these things, distributing to each one individually just as He wills***. "I Corinthians 12:7. However, these gifts are only reserved for those who diligently seek God. It is **not** for those who are 'trying-out God' to see if He works, fits into their lifestyle or, those who choose to remain indecisive towards Him.

"***So then because you are lukewarm, and neither cold or hot, I will spew you out of my mouth."*** Revelation 3:16. This verse is letting us know there is no such thing as middle ground with God; it's either all or none! Now let us go back and address what angered Jesus enough to boldly and publicly accuse the religious lawyers of deceit, hindrance and deprivation. The reason was that they were keeping ardent seekers of spiritual truth away from accessing the ultimate life changing system and person who is the Holy Spirit; He can now take up residence, not rest upon saints as He did in the Old Treaty.

Beloved, when you have access to God, you have everything! One of the most relevant and detailed example of having access to everything is the teaching of what most refer to as The Prodigal son. The son who chose to leave had access to everything his father had but chose to get his small portion and leave; the son who stayed also had access to everything but did not realize his privilege, rights or inheritance.

Again, the Holy Spirit is "**the key**" person who teaches and lets us realize that we **do** have access to God who owns everything! Wow! The Holy Spirit is available to guide, remind, empower, abide and teach citizens about the kingdom truths and entitlements. Beloved, a modern-day description for 'the key of knowledge' would be **'the grad-school of revelation that the Holy Spirit grants to mature believers which is not disclosed to grade school students**.'

In the Old Testament, the Holy Spirit would come to rest upon saints in order to partner with them to fulfill a particular work, perform a certain service or to disclose something prophetic. Upon completion, the Holy Spirit would depart. "…***And it came to pass, that, when the spirit rested upon them, they prophesied, and did not cease.***" Numbers 11:25. However, in the New Treaty, Jesus said, "***And I will pray the Father, and He shall give you another Comforter, that he may abide with you forever***..." John 14:16.

Again, in our present time, God's Holy Spirit will not depart unless we grieve Him in some way. However, The Word of God says, "***You shall receive power***…" Acts 1:8. Also, He will disclose to a specific citizen a word or provide healing to a particular person who is sincere and diligent. And, He will even reveal the status of a person to you. On the other hand, the Holy Spirit will convict the world of three things. "***And when He has come, He** –the Holy Spirit– **will convict the world of sin, and of righteousness, and of judgment:***" John 16:8. God's Holy Spirit is amazing and desires to work with the diligent!

The Role Transgression Plays in The Kingdom of God

In God's marvelous and brilliant administration *–His kingdom–* here on earth for the last two thousand years, there is one major hindrance which adversely impacts its dynamics. And, that is a clandestine transgression called **iniquity**.' We will clearly detail each one on the following pages in which we disclose there are five types of transgression, not sin. Sin just happens to be the lowest form of the five-types. As you know, the Word of Truth lists them as: sin, iniquity, unbelief, abomination and blaspheme.

As these five words seem to get bigger in syllables/letters, they grow more in severity than their predecessor as well. And, we are to always keep in mind that the only objective of ALL five types of transgression is to try and keep us in its revolving door of sensual pleasures, debauchery and selfishness. In other words, their central themes are to focus on self-indulgence and manipulation of others to get what we desire, lust after and crave; it's all about individualism not helping others to grow and mature.

The Scripture asks, "***But then what benefit did you get from the things of which you are now ashamed***?" Romans 6:21. NKJV. Let no one deceive you into thinking that there is **no** pleasure in sin; there certainly is! The Word of Life spells out, "***the pleasures of sin***..." Hebrews 11:25. Usually, it is only one person who is more pleased than the other participant!

As stated earlier, we realize the two most important designations/titles are stewards of God and ambassadors for Christ. This means there is information and requirements we must become more familiar with so that we can, "***be ready always to give an answer to every man that asks you a reason of the hope that is in you with meekness and fear.***"." I Peter 3:15. We are here to lift-up others so that we all benefit corporately and mature as one body. "***We then that are strong ought to bear the infirmities of the weak, and not to please ourselves.***" Romans 15:1. We have been taught that any deviation from God's Word or rule is called sin. This is not Biblically correct!

The Word of Truth says, "***For all have sinned, and come short of the glory of God***..." Romans 3:23. This is the open rejection of God's underserved favor called grace which is provided through the sacrifice of His only begotten son, Jesus the Christ. This is man's sin!

Further Unveiling of <u>Transgression</u>, ~~Not Sin~~!

Beloved of The Lord, over the last two thousand years, the church has generalized and misappropriated this small word, sin to be a monumental deviation from what is right and Godly. And, it has become a miscellaneous catch-all for every type of abnormality from God's Word, directives and expectations.

As you have heard/read, everything bad we do is limited or assigned the word sin; no matter what we engage in contrary to God's Word. Again, this is not precise! The Scripture totally disagrees with man's interpretation and watered-down version of sin and provides specific details on a much greater scale.

Again, God's Words clearly spell out a total of five (5) different types of **<u>transgression</u>** which are:

<u>sin</u>, **<u>iniquity</u>**, **<u>unbelief</u>**, **<u>abomination</u>** and **<u>blaspheme.</u>**

We would never say, all have committed **iniquity** against God.
Neither would we say, all have committed **unbelief** against God.
Neither would we say, all have committed **abomination** against God.
Finally, we would **<u>not</u>** say all have committed **blasphemy** against God.

However, we can correctly and appropriately state, "***for all have sinned, and come short of the glory of God.***" Romans 6:23. Now, let us detail each type in process for clarity and proper understanding.

1.<u>Sin</u>- is **<u>overt</u>** or plain to see; not much has to be mentioned or explained because it is the most common and obvious transgression of the five. Everyone knows sin as; stealing, lying, cursing, disobeying, and breaking God's commandments and the rejection of Jesus which has kept us out of alignment with God.

2. **Iniquity**- is **covert** or secretive which is not easily detected by anyone even in their midst; these include deviations like **un**-forgiveness, **jealousy**, envy, hatred and malice etc.; the evidence of these type transgressions may **not** be obvious or in plain sight but concealed within a person. Also, iniquity is so seductive that it can take up residence in someone we live with for decades and not ever be picked-up or uncovered by the closest friend, parents, sibling or spouse. These are weights and agony which God never designed humans to carry or live with. And, it is why His Word says, "***casting all your care upon Him, for He cares for you.***" I Peter 5:7. Furthermore, it was not sin or something overt Lucifer committed why he was cast out of Heaven, but iniquity. The Word points out, "***You were perfect in your ways from the day you were created, Till iniquity was found in you***." Ezekiel 28:15.

3. **Unbelief**- is both a **personal choice** and a private state of being. It can have adverse effects when engaging the Word of God. It too is clandestine in nature like iniquity. The Word of Life mentions of Jesus, "…***and He did not many mighty works there because of their unbelief.***." Matthew 13:58. You see beloved, unbelief tied the hands of God from providing sustenance that the people needed. Notice, it was not sin, iniquity, abomination or blasphemy that hindered Jesus but unbelief. Remember, it was unbelief that prevented the father of John the Baptist from speaking for nine months. See **Luke 1:13-20.**

4. **Abomination**- is an action which is **not concealed** and it repulses God above all the rest; this is when we deliberately deviate from the norm or standard i.e.: choosing to engage in an intimate perverse sexual relationship with animals or of the same sex. This includes sexual deviation, transgender, lesbianism and bestiality. "***You shall not lie with a male as with a woman. It is an abomination***." Lev. 18:22. However, there is still hope and forgiveness available; it is up to believers to pray and fast for those who God still loves; He loves them, not their deviation. In order to set them free of this web of entanglement and *–individualism–* which leads to sensual bondage, we are to gently guide them through meekness, counsel and by demonstrating a Godly lifestyle. This way, they see what true, acceptable and holy living is like to our Holy God.

5.**Blaspheme** means to **speak evil** and/or to attribute the works of the Holy Spirit as evil. This is **overt** and verbally expressed; it means to speak evil of what is sacred and presided over by His Holy Spirit. There are plans of restoration for the other four types but **not** for blasphemy. "***But he that shall blaspheme against the Holy Spirit has never forgiveness, but is in danger of eternal damnation***." Mark 3:29. The Holy Spirit is the only person in charge right now and with full authority; He is discreet and easily grieved yet, powerful and able to permanently indwell believers if they so desire. Remember, He first seals *–Eph. 1:13–* those who confess Jesus as Lord. This Means He:

S-tamps
E-veryone
A-sking *for*
L-ove &
S-alvation

This is the first things He does. The Word confirms, "***And do not grieve the Holy Spirit of God, by whom you were sealed for the day of redemption.***" Ephesians 4:30. As we've pointed out earlier, there is a vast difference between being sealed and being filled by Him!

Lust, The #1 Enemy of The Kingdom of God

"***For all that is in the world, the lust of the flesh, and the lust of the eyes, and the pride of life, is not of the Father, but is of the world***.".1 John 2:16. Contrary to what some people may have been taught, the devil or satan is NOT the major culprit believers face today; but it is lust which stands at the fore-front of most of believer's mind and personal life. Also, God's Word tells us "***...corruption that is in the world through lust***." II Peter 1:4.

This is our own lust, desires and cravings! Spiritually, the Word of God says it is a '**lack of knowledge**' that destroys us, not the devil. Hosea 4:6. Let us prove it by the Word of Truth how lust originates and who is responsible for its port of entry and arrival. Furthermore, we will dissect the following verse so that we have a clear understanding of how lust originates, develops and its conclusion. Jesus' half-brother, James pin-points lust as, "***13 Let no man say when he is tempted, I am tempted of God: for God cannot be tempted with evil, neither temps He any man: 14 But every man is tempted, when he is drawn away of his own lust, and enticed. 15 Then when lust has conceived, it brings forth sin: and sin, when it is finished, brings forth death***. James 1:13-15. Beloved, when we look at the primary words in this verse, it provides explicit details as follows:

1-"but every man is tempted,
2- when he is drawn away of his own lust,
3- and enticed.
4- Then when lust hath conceived,
5- it brings forth sin: and sin when it is finished
6- brings forth death." James 1:14-15.

The six (**6**) underlined words carries great insight and depth in stunning details. We can no longer blame the enemy for our error and adverse situation because God's Word shifts the responsibility on us. Also, Jesus spells out thirteen (**13**) major hindrances which can greatly affect all of us. "***For from within, out of the heart*** –sub-conscious mind– ***of men, proceed:***

1-evil thoughts ie: you allow your mind to entertain ungodly things
2-adulteries............ie: sex outside of a man & woman in marriage
3-fornications ....ie: any type of sex while **un**-married
4-murders ....ie: taking a human life; including your own
5-thefts........................... ie: taking of another person's goods
6-covetousness...........ie: greed, saving/keeping only for yourself
7-wickedness ....ie: oppressing the poor/being mean
8-deceit ....ie: to intentionally mislead
9-lasciviousness..........ie; extreme indulgence in sensual pleasures
10-an evil eye.........................ie: being envious/nasty or unkind
11-blasphemy..............ie: speak evil of what is Godly; to slander
12-pride ....ie: arrogance, exalting yourself; exaggerate
13-foolishness.......................ie; lack of reasonable moral sense

All these evil things come from within, and defile the man." Mark 7:21-23. Did you notice #1 which further substantiates the primary Key? It is from the above list that lust is birthed and begins to invite evil things to support **our own lust** as stated above in our Covenant.

However, let's move to an even higher level and address the LOVE and lust arena from three (3) perspectives. First, we created acronyms for all three in order to show both the details and provide the right description. They outline **God's** view, the **believer's** outlook and finally, the **world's** perception of love.

They are as follows:

A -------------------------------**B** -----------------------------**C**

God	**The Believer**	**World**
L-egally	**L**-earn	**L**-ive
O-wns &	**O**-ne's	**U**-nder
V-alues	**V**-ery	**S**-ensual
E-very(one) thing	**E**-xistence	**T**-houghts

As you can see, **LOVE** from God's vantage point is vastly different than how the world spells love. The world misconstrues **LUST** for love. This is why you hear 'love' being used so rampantly in every situation. Another common misconception is that hate is the opposite of love; this is not true! It is **lust** that is the opposite of **love**. Lust is generally fulfilling only one person's desire at the expense of another. This is **always** the case! In other words, lust goes one-way; true love is a two-way street!

On the other hand, love depicts God completeness because He **L**egally **O**wns and **V**alues **E**veryone and everything, not their transgression. God gave His one and only Son which no parent would sacrifice today! The Godly type of Love is unselfish and is like a bi-lateral contract; there are two parties with the same mutual interests. This is why we think of love from our own perspective, it is generally about obtaining not giving or sacrificing.

However, as believers, we are to step up and Learn One's Very Existence. In essence, when we learn who we are *–which is spelled out in chapter one on page #9–* we will place a higher value on others and love them in a Godly way. We know there are other types of love such as eros/sensual, storge/fondness, philia/bond between friends and **Agape** which is the God kind *–unconditional–* that counts!

The Role Angels Play in The Kingdom

There have been widespread rumors, speculations and teachings as to the role angels play in believer's life today. Let us address some of those misunderstandings and provide you with some historical examples as well as Scriptural insight. In the Old Treaty, angels provided a "***hedge of protection***" for saints –**Job 1:10**– and were referred to and called "***sons of God***." **Job 38:7**. However, in the new Treaty this term "sons of God" is directed ONLY to believers. See John 1:12, Galatians 3:26 & 4:6 and I John 3:1.

Did you remember when Jesus was weak after being tempted, "…***angels ministered unto Him.***" Mark 1:13? As far as new believers today, the first thing angels recognize are those who confess Jesus. As a result, they enjoy a time of great celebration about each one who repents. "***Likewise, I say to you, there is joy in the presence of the angels of God over one sinner who repents***." Luke 15:10. John told us, "***But as many as received Him, to them gave He power to become the sons of God, even to them that believe on His name***."John1:12.

Jesus, John and Paul all confirmed this title "***sons of God***." to be accurate. Also, visitations were made to Joseph and Mary. Some angels even freed believers in the New Treaty who are falsely imprisoned. "***And, behold, the angel of the Lord came upon him, and a light shined in the prison: and he smote Peter on the side, and raised him up, saying, Arise up quickly. And his chains fell off from his hands***." Acts 12:7. Also, in relationship to believers today, angels are referred to as ministering spirits. "…***are they not all ministering spirits sent forth to minister for those who will inherit salvation***?" Hebrews 1:14. It is critical to point out that if you ever think you see an angel of God, there is a two or three-word sequence which they must say to clarify they are indeed from God; those special words are "**fear not** or, **do not fear**" which is mentioned from the book of Genesis to the end of The Revelation of Jesus Christ. Beloved, in almost every angel encounter with a human, this phrase was preceded before the message was mentioned.

God gave us all a heads-up regarding His angels as well as those of our adversary –satan– and his demons. It is unique to point out that most major religious founders claim to have a message or visitation from/by an angel, not from God. And, the message those 'angels' brought either added something or changed The Word of Truth to suit their own individualistic view.

God's Word exposes the enemy and says, "***and no wonder! for satan himself transforms himself into an angel of light***." II Corinthians 11:14. Why do you think he cloaks himself as an angel? Is it **only** to appear supernatural, change our direction from Jesus or to deceive! We know, as smart, dynamic and powerful as God's angels are, they do not fully comprehend the whole concept of the Gospel. Neither do they understand the salvation process of man through Jesus whom they worship. Peter confirmed it by stating, ***"...those who have preached the gospel to you by the Holy Spirit sent from Heaven—things which angels desire to look into***." 1 Peter 1:12 Another critical perspective to detail is that angels provide a 'hedge of protection' for infants regardless of religious beliefs, denominational position or parent's stance.

One final note and summary, in the Old Treaty the angels of God carried out specific duties *–Isaiah 37:36*, - and were messengers. Evidence of which was clearly seen in Genesis, Daniel 10:11-13, Isaiah, The Psalms and many other books. The title or status for all who confess Jesus as Lord are called and should now be referred to as "**sons of God**." "***Behold what manner of love the Father has bestowed upon us that we should be called the sons of God***." I John 3:1. Then, God mentions how He sees His Offspring. "***And because you are sons, God has sent forth the Spirit of His son into our hearts crying, Abba Father***." Galatians 4:6.

The (4) - or- (9) Key Factors of the Great Commission

We are the beloved of Abba, Elohim and Adonai –which means, '**My Lord** and the plural of **Majesty**.' The greatest asset which we are to pursue and experience immediately after confessing Jesus as Lord of our life is to desire the baptism of the Holy Spirit. What exactly is this baptism which John said is greater than his own? It was clearly spelled out and was written which one ranks above the other so that we will know which takes precedence; John said:

(1)--"***I indeed baptize you with water unto repentance,***
(2)--*but He who is coming after me is mightier than I, whose sandals I am not worthy to carry.*
(3)--He will baptize you with the Holy Spirit and fire." Matt. 3:11.

The first thing we are to realize is that there are two baptisms. The next thing we are to ask ourselves is, what is the baptism of fire? Today this verse and term seems to be deliberately avoided, rarely mentioned and consciously excluded in most teachings. As you can see above, there is a clear distinction and a tremendous difference it made in Jesus' baptism with the Holy Spirit and fire as compared with that of John's baptism by the physical H_2O, water.

The Word of Life says, "***For as many as are led by the Spirit of God, they are the sons of God***. "Romans 8:14. Beloved, this was the unveiling or administration which Isaiah saw hundreds of years' prior of Messiah's arrival. "...***and the government will be upon His shoulder. And His name will be called Wonderful Counselor, Mighty God, Everlasting Father, Prince of Peace. Of the increase of His government and peace there will be no end***." Isaiah 9:6-7.

Some citizens today have come to grips with the reality that Jesus really brought an entire administration (*see illustration bottom of page #9*) which is designed to take the place of the old administration. First, let us go back and lay the proper foundation. Whenever a king, an important leader of a country or sovereignty is about to arrive, the city, state or country make provisions and are in anticipation of their appearance. This arrival is usually heralded by a great announcement or a forerunner whether by word-of mouth, TV or flyer alluding to their debut. This also means to shift the focus from the messenger to the highly anticipated person. In other words, there should be no misunderstanding of who is the highly exalted person.

Today, we have exchanged the fore-runner –John– for The King who is Jesus. And, John's baptism is proclaimed and has taken precedence over Jesus' Baptism with the "Holy Spirit and fire." Matt. 3:11. If you doubt me, call and ask someone "were you baptized with the Holy Spirit and fire, or were you baptized in water? When I ask this question, it primarily stops at John's Baptism. We are not minimizing John's baptism we are exalting Jesus' spiritual and superior Baptism.

Today, just about all sects incorporate some form of John's baptism which almost every religion acknowledges and hold it dear to themselves as special and distinguishable date. Also, ministers identify water baptism in some form, fashion, ritual or ceremony as a benchmark to show identification with Christ and of a change.

There is also another popular message which most evangelical group uses and quote to spread their outreach ministry. This is a widely recognized term and primarily quoted from the book of Matthew and **<u>not</u>** Mark's account which is far more detailed and precise rendition. We are eluding to "**The Great Commission**." Matthew's version encompasses only four (4) main points and spelled out as follows:

1.***Go therefore and make disciples of all the nations***
2. baptizing them in the name of the Father, Son and Holy Spirit,
3. teaching them to observe all things that I have commanded you;
4. and lo, I am with you always, even to the end of the age."
Amen." Matthew 28:19-20

This is very direct and straight forward! However, let's take a look at Mark's more detailed and eye-opening account which consist of nine (9) stunning points." ***And He said to them:***

1..Go into all the world and preach the gospel to every creature.
2..He who believes and is baptized will be saved;
3..but he who does not believe will be condemned.

4..And these signs will follow those who believe:
5..In My name they will cast out demons;
6..they will speak with new tongues; (**dialect**)

*7.. **they will take up serpents;***
8..and if they drink anything deadly, it will by not hurt them
9..they will lay hands on the sick, and they will recover."
Mark 16:15-18.

Beloved, which of the two accounts do you think The Lord desires us to pay closer attention to and disseminate? Let's observe what took place immediately after Mark's detailed description. It concludes in verses nineteen and twenty,

1--"***So then, after the Lord had spoken to them,***
2--He was received up into Heaven,
3--and sat down at the right hand of God.
4--And they went out and preached everywhere,
5--the Lord working with them and confirming the word through the accompanying signs." Amen.

"Please note, there is a VAST difference between both Matthew's account and Mark's description. One Sunday morning I was attending a Bible Study right before the 11 o'clock service. The person teaching the class was ministering on The Great Commission. After he concluded, I raised my hand and asked the following question. "Why do we hold the teaching of the great commission by Matthew, when Mark *–who provided a more detailed description–* wrote his gospel first?" I did not know that by asking this question it would later get me thrown out of the class and almost arrested the following week.

When I attended church that following Sunday, if I would have stayed in the church building, a police officer told me, "*if I stayed, I stand the risk of being arrested for interrupting a religious service.*" I mentioned, a police officer tapped me on my shoulder while seated in the sanctuary before service and told me, "the law in North Carolina is that if you disrupt a religious service, you stand the risk of being arrested." Needless to say, I was curious and simply asked the question out of my own curiosity and interest. It was not intended to embarrass or put the minister *–who I spoke to earlier–* on the spot.

The reason we are distinguishing these areas of significance is that we would like to place things in God's proper order. Let us take a closer look into what is written as one of our primary pursuits. "***Till we all come in the unity of the faith, and of the knowledge of the Son of God, unto a perfect man, unto the measure of the stature of the fullness of Christ.***" Ephesians 4:13. It is critical that we all get on the same page of understanding, avoid denominational teachings and personal interpretation. As citizens of Heaven on earth, our goal, direction and pursuit should primarily be the administration of God.

Remember, Jesus said "***but seek first the kingdom of God and His righteousness and all these things shall be added unto you.***" Matthew 6:33. Every other topic or subject should come in a distant second. There is no greater subject to track-down, read or study than the kingdom of God! Jesus' priority and directive about pursuing the kingdom should be paramount!

'Some Deceived Citizen's Outlook'

Everyone living right now in the United States realize they are in a country. And, we know a country is defined as **a nation with its own government occupying a particular territory**. In the kingdom of God, it is a similar state but at the same time drastically different in its administrations. How do we enter this kingdom? It is by our belief and confession of Jesus as Lord which allows us to enter through the **Door** into the kingdom. Jesus said, "…***I am the Door.***" John 10:9.

Once we enter, we can participate in the rights and privileges of His domain/territory using keys which provides access into other areas. However, the Scripture tells us there are believers who engage in transgression and consider themselves Christians, children of God, saved, and born again. God gave '**eviction notices as seen below**.' God's Word clearly points out in detail, ***"do you not know that;***

1--the unrighteous will not inherit 'the kingdom of God?'
2--Do not be deceived, neither fornicators ---all kinds of sexual sins
3--nor idolaters ---------------------- worship or serve any false gods
4--nor adulterers ---------------- having sex outside a Godly marriage
5--nor homosexuals ---------- engage in lesbianism or homosexuality
6--nor sodomites --------------------- anal sex with people or animals
7--nor thieves, ----------------------- those who deceives & rob others
8--nor covetous, ---------------------- desire what others have; grudge
9--nor drunkards, ------------------- use of alcohol, beer to get a buzz
10--nor revilers, ------------ those who curse & use abusive language
11--nor extortioners ------------------ shakedown; money for service

will inherit the kingdom of God. I Corinthians 6:9-10. "***And such were some of you. But you were washed, but you were sanctified, but you were justified in the name of the Lord Jesus and by the Spirit of our God.***" I Corinthians 6:11. In other words saint, some people may identify themselves as a Christian but they are not in the kingdom according to God's Word. Please read **Mark 10:17-25** about the rich young ruler. You can be good in deeds but have the wrong mentality.

The worst type of deception is not being duped by others or even the enemy, but it is self-deception. Therefore, let us **not** continue to mislead ourselves to think we can still hold on to the past and engage in the new rights and privileges as citizens in God's awesome kingdom dynamics. We are not to conduct ourselves as we did when we were engaged in all types of sensual pleasures in the world.

The same adherence and submission we yielded to our employer's directives are the same basic requirements for being in the kingdom. At the pinnacle of our job description is that we must choose to **forgive** right away and to **love** unconditionally. And, by doing so, we will be exercising discipline throughout our daily lives which allows us to be very effective in both worlds! God forgave; we are to forgive! it's His directive!

How satan Received The kingdoms of The World & Earth's Splendor

Over the next four pages, we will unveil a deep seldom mentioned spiritual secret. We will also provide a condensed and detailed description of earth along with how satan acquired the kingdoms of the world. As we know, God created Lucifer, NOT satan. Lucifer rebelled and became satan. God created all things through Jesus Christ including all Heavenly beings ie; Arc-angels, Cherubim, Seraphim, the four living beings, Heavenly hosts and angels.

Lucifer was an anointed cherub who directed the music and worship towards God. It was by his adverse thoughts and jealousy why Lucifer fell and became satan. As we know, any act of personal rebellion against God or His Word will cause a designation change as well as a status alteration. For example, the Prophet Ezekiel provided us with both Lucifer's history *–before recorded time–* and what his job description was while he was in Heaven but prior to his fall. There were nine (9) points made about him.

1--"*You were in Eden, the garden of God;*
2--*Every precious stone was your covering:*
3--*The sardius, topaz, and diamond, Beryl, onyx, and jasper, Sapphire, turquoise, and emerald with gold.*

4--*The workmanship of your timbrels and pipes was prepared for you on the day you were created.*

5--*you were the anointed cherub who covers; I established you;*
6--*You were on the holy mountain of God;*
7--*You walked back and forth in the midst of fiery stones.*
8--*you were perfect in your ways from the day you were created,*
9--*Till <u>iniquity</u> was found in you*." Ezekiel 28:13-15.

What was found in him? Iniquity, not sin! Iniquity is a whole other topic all on its own. However, let's move forward. The primary reason Lucifer was cast out of Heaven began with his thought processes which brought about jealousy. Further details were provided by the Prophet Isaiah who stated;

1-- "***For you have said in your <u>heart</u>,***
2--*<u>I will</u>* ***ascend into heaven,***
3--*<u>I will</u>* ***exalt my throne above the stars of God:***
4--*<u>I will</u>* ***sit also upon the mount of the congregation, in the sides of the north;***
5--*<u>I will</u>* ***ascend above the heights of the clouds;***
6--*<u>I will</u>* ***be like the Most High***." Isaiah 14:13-14.

As soon as these five thoughts *–above–* were almost complete, satan was instantly fired for insubordination and cast out of Heaven along with the 1/3 of God angels whom chose to follow him; they became demons. The earth is the only living planet in the universe that God made and gave to Adam to have dominion over <u>all</u> its magnificence. When satan realized he had nothing *–after being thrown out of Heaven–* he tested Adam and Eve of the **knowledge** God gave them; we know they failed the test miserably.

All that God had given to Adam and Eve was immediately deeded over to this unemployed Cherub who is now the god of this world's system. **See II Corinthians 4:4**. Adam's fall was due primarily to the fact that he did not realize who he was. What was the infraction Adam committed, it was treason? **<u>Treason</u>** is the crime of betraying one's country. Adam's fall relinquished the rights and privileges which came as earth's owner. Also, he had God's glory and first-hand knowledge of all his circumstance. We know this because when the tempter came to Adam and Eve *–who were the legal owners of this magnificent planet–* they did not cherish who they were associated with; neither did he value or call on God for assistance. There was and still is wealth beyond imagination of earth's magnificent hidden treasures.

The fallen cherub, now called satan/deceiver, felt good knowing he had territory, property, access to a splendid domain and a beautiful region filled with glory, wealth and magnificence. We know this because when he tempted Jesus approximately four-thousand years later, he offered Him what he now owned legally which includes earth's wealth, riches and brilliance. This desire for wealth is the primary problem with humans, even today. Even though we have been restored to the state of being the 'righteousness of God in Christ' ***–II***

Corinthians 5:21– some do not value or take this new status with God seriously. This is why some still say, "I am a sinner and a servant" when they are really sons of God and friends of Jesus. As beautiful as the planet Saturn is with its striking colors, brilliant rigs and illustriousness beauty, some believe earth was much more stunning, radiant and far more spectacular in every way when God initially created it! Why, because God was here!

Mature offspring of God today realize that the devil could not offer or tempt Jesus with something he did not own. "***Then the devil, taking Him up on a high mountain, showed Him all the kingdoms of the world in a moment of time. And the devil said to Him, "All this authority I will give You, and their glory; for this has been delivered to me, and I give it to whomever I wish. Therefore, if You will worship before me, all will be Yours"*** Luke 4:5-7.

At some point in time, this same offer will be presented to a human who will be blown away by earth's magnificence, abundant wealth and desire its glory. And, as a result, he will both rule and deceive the whole world; he will be called the anti-Christ. ***"He performs great signs, so that he even makes fire come down from heaven on the earth in the sight of men."*** Revelation 13:13.

God's Primary Solution for All; including the Poor

Beloved, what you are about to read and recognize is man's most common problem which was both addressed and resolved by Jesus. We are referring to the poor and their condition. Do you remember when John the Baptist was arrested and put in prison; he sent his disciples to ask Jesus, ***"are You the Coming One, or do we look for another? Jesus answered and said to them***
1-Go and tell John the things which you hear and see
2-the blind see and
3-the lame walk;
4-the lepers are cleansed and
5-the deaf hear;
6-the dead are raised up and
7-the poor have 'the gospel' preached to them." Matthew 11:3-5.

Jesus spelled out that it is not money the poor needs to solve their problem but a new direction and an administration. In other words, His answer was to point people to **the gospel**/Good News surrounding His Kingdom. God is clearly spelling out His ultimate solution *–not just for the poor–* but for earth's turmoil which includes everyone. Again, the answer to every need is the Kingdom's dynamics headed-up by His Holy Spirit. Remember, a new administration is what Jesus brought to earth according to the Prophet Isaiah. "***Of the increase of His government and peace there will be no end*.**" Isaiah 9:6-7.

This is why during Jesus' brief ministry, He gave His Disciples specific instructions on what they are to announce where ever they go; "***as you go, preach saying the kingdom of God has arrived.***" Matthew 10:7. The message everyone needs to know more about in order to experience God's peace and security in their lives is now accessible. Also, this '**Good News**' is designed to provide keys, insight and authority over principalities, powers and rulers of darkness of this world. There are much more details spelled out by the Apostle Paul in Ephesians chapter six.

Over the years, most of us have come to realize that the solution to problems is **not** religion, traditions, or money but a lack of knowledge and a better relationship with Our Creator. Money provides a temporary fix to an on-going problem but it is not a permanent answer for prolonged success. Jesus said He was leaving His peace which is defined as 'the absence of frustration.' "***Peace I leave with you, my peace I give unto you: not as the world giveth, give I unto you. Let not your heart be troubled, neither let it be afraid***." John 14:27. Later on the Apostle Paul confirmed and supported Jesus' statement above. "***And the peace of God, which passes all understanding, shall keep your hearts and minds through Christ Jesus***." Philippians 4:7. Once again, please refer to the diagram about heart on page #8.

You see beloved, God's Word will calm our subconscious mind, provide peace for clear thinking and solutions for effective living. This include steps the poor can take despite their previous choices. The new choice everyone can make is to learn more about what God has put in place for His offspring and use His spiritual principles to obtain natural results. This is why Jesus prioritizes and spells out for us what we are to go after first! "***but seek first the kingdom of God and His righteousness and all these things shall be added unto you***." Matthew. 6:33. It is evident that Jesus' directive is for fulfillment, peace of mind and a better lifestyle which can be made available to anyone who chooses to come to God through Jesus. In essence, Jesus said all the things we need today are in one place and it stems from one **source**!

When someone confess Jesus as Lord or, if they choose to **re**commit their lifestyle by pursuing His directive, they will be able to partake in God's government. Let's prove it; do you recall when Phillip in Acts chapter nine went to minister to the city of Samaria? There was Simon the sorcerer who bewitched the people with all kinds of evil deeds. "***But when they believed Philip as he preached the things concerning the kingdom of God and the name of Jesus Christ, both men and women were baptized. Then Simon himself also believed; and when he was baptized he continued with Philip, and was amazed, seeing the miracles and signs which were done***." Acts 8:12-13.

When the city of Samaria was won over to The Lord, what message did Phillip proclaim in that city? It was the administration of God and the name of Jesus. Even though Simon, now converted and marveled at the great spectacles and the abundant signs which was far superior to anything he was used to seeing, he desired to embrace God's new dynamic workings and **not** go back into drugs, trickery and his old magician's ploy.

Beloved, God's awe-inspiring works become evident by the administrator of God –*His Holy Spirit*– who works hand-in-hand with the use of the matchless name of Jesus. Again, this is the right combination that the poor in our city and state across the country needs so they become more engaged. It is not membership they need but familiarization with God's administration in order to deal with their personal problems.

Chapter VII
The Nine (9) "Blessings of The Kingdom of God," ~~not The Beatitudes~~!

Saints of God and Joint heirs with Christ, of all the things we wrote, this is the pinnacle of what we are to embrace and memorize. And, we are about to clear up a simple misunderstanding which has both been renamed and overlooked for generations. We are referencing what has been widely called, The Beatitudes." The correct title should be 'The Nine (9) **Blessings** of the Kingdom' stated by Matthew concerning Jesus' awesome teaching on this subject; they are:

*1-Blessed are the poor in spirit; for theirs is the **kingdom** of heaven.*
2- Blessed are they that mourn: for they shall be comforted.
3- Blessed are the meek: for they shall inherit the earth.
4- Blessed are they which do hunger and thirst after righteousness: for they shall be filled.
5- Blessed are the merciful: for they shall obtain mercy.
6- Blessed are the pure in heart: for they shall see God.
7- Blessed are the peacemakers: for they shall be called the children of God.
8- Blessed are they which are persecuted for righteousness' sake: for theirs is the kingdom of heaven.
9 Blessed are you, when men shall revile you, and persecute you, and shall say all manner of evil against you falsely, for my sake.

In verse twelve it concludes, ***"Rejoice, and be exceeding glad: for great is your reward in heaven: for so persecuted they the prophets which were before you."*** Matthew 5:3-12. The word beatitude comes from the Latin word 'beatus' meaning both "happy" and "blessed." However, it is NOT a word used by Jesus or Matthew. Again, let us stick to God's Word and appropriate all nine by Jesus as, '**The Blessings of His Kingdom**' and not 'the attitudes to be.' As you know, it is commonly mentioned today and erroneous retitled by others in the past. God is all about disseminating accurate information which we are to realize, grasp and meditate on daily.

What Now; What Do You Do as of Today?

First, do not look back at what you used to do; but face forward. ***"...But Jesus said to him, no one, having put his hand to the plow, and looking back, is fit for the kingdom of God.*"** Luke 9:62. Beloved of Abba, now that you have seen the kingdom dynamics in a whole new light with its available nine (9) **blessings**, nine (9 **keys** nine (9) **gifts**, your greatest approach is to embrace all its magnificence.

Then, put **everything** you know in second place and "...***seek first the kingdom of God and His righteousness***..." Matthew 6:33. This is your primary directive by Jesus who said you are to pursue, open and become familiar. Not only is the kingdom your most important pursuit after coming to Christ, but it is now accessible!

After putting into practice some; preferably all of its keys, realize that you are His **steward.** You are also given daily responsibilities to carry out which is why He calls you an **ambassador**. Therefore, you proudly represent Christ where ever you go. You know that you are the righteousness of God in Him. Review page **27**. Remember your personal and premier assignment which is, "***...he who wins souls is wise***." Proverbs 11:30. This becomes your mission to introduce Christ and His **Good News** of the kingdom to others.

It is imperative that you realize, your most valuable asset to God is your **thought life**. Let us take a look at Paul's directive to the church at Corinth; he said, "***casting down imaginations and every high thing that exalts itself against the knowledge of God and bringing into captivity every thought to the obedience of Christ***. II Corinthians 10:5. Remember, '**forgiveness** and **love**' **(#9)** are combined keys which sits at the pinnacle of kingdom's principles.

The Word of Life says, "***Owe no man anything, but to love one another: for he that loves another hath fulfilled the law***." Romans 13:8. Our only debt to others is genuine love. Now that we are born of God, it means we are born to love the unloved and even those who hate and dislikes us; we are to speak and say nice things about them.

As you know, another vital key is that you are to maintain **humility (#5)** so that God will exalt you. "***Therefore <u>humble</u> yourselves under the mighty hand of God, that He may exalt you in due time***." 1 Peter 5:6. Finally, you are to spend time with God early so He gets the memo before your daily activities begin. This way, angels can legally act in the spirit realm for you. The ultimate clincher starts as you thank God **<u>in</u>** everything *–not **<u>for</u>** everything–* you are involved in on a daily basis.

"***Therefore, since we are receiving a kingdom which <u>cannot be shaken</u>, let us have grace, by which we may serve God acceptably with reverence and godly fear***." Hebrews 12:28. And, you are to embrace all these new insights in the matchless name of **<u>Jesus</u>**!

Next Step about what you've just heard or read?

As a believer in Jesus The Christ, the most critical step you are to take as of today is to start thanking God for what His **<u>Holy Spirit</u>** can do; He is our primary Source of information and the only assigned teacher of God's Word. Seminaries, Bible studies, your pastor, teachers and Bible School provide secondary means of insight. We listed some of His works on pages **15-17, 19-21 and 51-58.**

Please give up television one of the seven days to **meditate**. Psalms 1:1-3. I Tim. 4:15. By employing these steps, it will begin to carve-out a new mind–set of **<u>thanksgiving</u>** and **<u>recognition</u>** of who He is! You can do so while driving, at leisure, during your devotion time or simply acknowledge God's presence by His Awesome Holy Spirit.

<u>This way, **He** can</u>:		**<u>He also:</u>**
<u>G</u> uide you into all truth	John 14:26-27	**<u>G</u>**ives
<u>R</u> emind you of all things	John 16:7; 13	**<u>U</u>**nique
<u>E</u> mpower you to do His works	Acts 1:8	**<u>I</u>**nstructions &
<u>A</u> bide in you; God's temple	1 Cor.6:18	**<u>D</u>**etails
<u>T</u> each you **<u>all</u>** things	John 14:26-27	**<u>E</u>**veryday

"Your Golden Rule Commitment"

In your personal quiet time, speak to your Lord *–owner–* God and say, "in the matchless name of Jesus I come to you believing the Good News of your Kingdom which was spelled-out just for me; You knew I would be right here today before the foundations of the world."

1 –I realize I don't belong to myself anymore; You are my owner.

2--I will begin spending quality time with You early in the morning.

3--One day-a-week I will fast TV, music, sensual pleasures, food for a ½ day to spend that quality time with You for disciplinary/health reasons.

4--I will raise up my hands and praise You; I will be kind, friendly and minister to others about Your glorious Kingdom; I ardently desire to be instructed by Your Awesome Holy Spirit from this ____day of____________ 20_ _ forward in the mighty name of Jesus.

<u>For Salvation</u> or to Pursue the Reason Why You are here

Father, in the name of Jesus, I realize more than ever that my life has a divine purpose because I am now identified with You, Your angels rejoiced about my decision to confess you as Owner. **Luke 15:10**. *Also, I understand that I am to live* ***<u>humbly</u>*** *before you and that my life is now hid with Christ in You.* **Colossians 3:3**. *By faith, I know You have revealed to me the purpose for my existence here on the earth which is to make a difference to my generation. In Jesus name.* ***What you have just read is a GPS; God's <u>P</u>lan of <u>S</u>alvation!***

Those who desire <u>both</u> baptisms, please read: Matthew 3:11.

Beloved, if you were given a multiple choice question as follows: **"As a believer of God's eternal Truth, which of the four choices regarding 'faith' would you accept, choose and desire today?"**

A—Little faith
B—Faith
C—Great faith
D—Most Holy Faith

I believe the majority of citizens would vie for choice '**D**.' Why, because we would like the best from God; isn't that true? This term is only mentioned once throughout God's entire Library in the book of **Jude** verse twenty; '**most holy faith**' is used when involved in unseen activities of the spiritual world. Also, there are supporting insights of this spiritual communication mentioned in **Acts 19:1-6, Romans 8:26-27, I Cor. 14:2, 14** and v: **39**. Also, please read the entire tenth chapter of **Daniel**; this example reveals the spiritual activities and battles *–behind the scenes–* in high places. Whether we acknowledge, use or deny its existence, we are no more or less a child of God. This communication is in a mystery *–**I Cor.** 14:4–* directly to God and seems to be more advanced than our English. On your own, you can ask God to provide further insight into this spiritual petition. The Scripture refers to it as 'praying in the spirit'. Again, **Ephesians 6:18**.

Your (4) Brand New Mind-set & Outlook!

1st--<u>C</u>ontrol your ***<u>thoughts</u>*** because it will **create** your words.
2nd--<u>C</u>hoose your ***<u>words</u>*** carefully because they will **reveal** your character.
3rd--<u>G</u>uard your ***<u>character</u>*** because it will control your **destiny**.
4th--Finally, **<u>Y</u>OU** determine your own ***<u>destiny</u>*** because there you will spend **eternity**.

Please review pages 56, 58, 63--66 for your daily applications!

The Seven (7) Criterion to Determine if you're in The Kingdom.

First**, let us start-out right away by stating, if you ***confess Jesus as **Lord** *–who is your* ***owner***– it means you are born again and **in** the Kingdom! **Romans 10:9-10**. Beloved, just as there are expectations, directives, timelines on a job, so too are instructions in God's Kingdom to carry-out. In other words, you can be just an employee for years or decades and still be in the company/kingdom; or, you could be promoted through knowledge of their guidelines to teach or oversee others which is by choice. How effective you become in the kingdom is solely determined by you. Some believe God will ask every believer two critical and direct questions: page #50. They are:

1--What have you done with the keys I gave you?
2--Give an account of your stewardship!

After accepting and coming in through The **Door** ***–who is Jesus–*** ***John. 10:9***– His Holy Spirit provide the keys which opens and operates The Kingdom. This is where stewardship responsibilities are spelled-out and ambassador's assignments are to be applied. Page 27.

Second**, but in conjunction with the first, Jesus gave us His directive; "...seek first the kingdom of God and His righteousness and all these things shall be added unto you***." Matt. 6:33. In concurrence with seeking the kingdom dynamics and choosing to maintain right standings, Jesus said, "...***whosoever will come after me, let him deny himself, and take up his cross, and follow me***." Mark 8:34. This will not be easy because we have our weekly work agenda planned, previous hobbies, and personal agendas which we committed to keep. In other words, God was only reserved for couple hours on Sunday if no major ball-game was on or sports activity was in town!

*__Third__, is **_obedience_** Jesus said, ***"But why do you call Me 'Lord, Lord,' and not do the things which I say?"*** Luke 6:46. We are to heed God's instructions and directives without denominational lenses. This is how we ***"...bear much fruit."*** John 15:8.

*__Fourth__, you practice the top key which is #9. As you recall, this is **_forgiveness_** *and* **_love_**; which you **CANNOT** do one without the other. Included in the forgiveness mandate Jesus clearly demonstrated the seventy times seven teaching. And, we are to love one another genuinely. These combined keys require there are no iniquity *–secret sin–* in you like; malice, envy, jealousy, not a gram of prejudice, greed, secret sexual/ungodly passions or desires you may be hiding. These will result in serious malfunctions. Please read **Matt. 7:21-23**.

*__Fifth__ is **_humility_** *–the middle key–* which is also the 5th key we mentioned earlier. In order for God to exalt you, you are to humble yourself and even 'take wrong.' "***Now therefore there is utterly a fault among you, because you go to law one with another. Why do you not rather take wrong? Why do you not rather suffer yourselves to be defrauded***?" 1 Corinthians 6:7.

*__Sixth__ is plain, direct and clearly spelled out. "***Do you not know that the unrighteous will not inherit the kingdom of God? Do not be deceived. Neither fornicators, nor idolaters, nor adulterers, nor homosexuals, nor sodomites, nor thieves, nor covetous, nor drunkards, nor revilers, nor extortioners will inherit the kingdom of God. And such were some of you, but you were washed, but you were sanctified, but you were justified in the name of the Lord Jesus and by the Spirit of our God***." I Corinthians. 6:9-11.

*Finally, **number seven** is, "***Now the works of the flesh are evident, which are: adultery fornication, uncleanness, lewdness, idolatry, sorcery, hatred, contentions, jealousies, outbursts of wrath, selfish ambitions, dissensions, heresies, envy, murders, drunkenness, revelries, and the like; of which I tell you beforehand, just as I also told you in time past, that those who practice such things will not inherit the kingdom of God.***" Galatians 5:19-21.

Let's summarize the seven sections; first, if you ****confess** Jesus as Lord, *seek the kingdom, *deny yourself, *obey His Word, this is mandatory, *forgive & love, *humble yourself do *NOT re-engage in the past lustful pleasures and do *NOT practice these in #7 above, you are in God's Kingdom.* **Welcome aboard!............**

What if you are engaged in one or more of the things listed in #6 & #7; what are you to do right now? Ask The Lord to forgive you and turn from it; "***but if we confess our sins to Him, He is faithful and just to forgive us our sins and to cleanse us from all unrighteousness.***" I John 1:9. You know this means **not** to re-turn or pick-up any of those activities. "***As a dog returns to its vomit, so a fool repeats his foolishness***." Proverbs 26:11.

Do you remember what God said to the Church at Laodicea? "***So then, because you are lukewarm, and neither cold nor hot, I will vomit you out of My mouth.***" Revelation 3:16. God is **jealous** and wants you all to Himself! This is why He told us the purpose He created man. "***Let us hear the conclusion of the whole matter: Fear God, and keep his commandments: for this is the whole duty of man***." Eccl. 12:13.

The author's personal prayer for you, the reader.

Abba, Father, I thank you for your amazing Holy Spirit *–who is now joined to the reader's spirit–* to teach them **GREAT** things like how to live an acceptable lifestyle and to pray effectively. I ask that He reminds them of the keys they have access to and the new information they have now realized about themselves. I thank you that their on-going relationship with You will be fine-tuned and more consistent. This is because Your Holy Spirit is available to **GUIDE** them by:

G-iving
U-nique
I-nstructions &
D-etails
E-veryday

to walk in confidence with You from this day forward. Remind them that they are the glory of **You** on earth who are created in **Your** image and likeness to function like You. And, I ask this in the unparalleled name of **Jesus** the Christ!

"***Therefore, since we are receiving a kingdom which cannot be shaken, let us have grace, by which we may serve God acceptably with reverence and Godly fear."*** Hebrews 12:28. In Jesus name!

AFC, *Paul. Vickers*

AFC, Paul Vickers

Your new confession is "***But as truly as I live, all the earth shall be filled with the glory of the Lord.***" Numbers 14:21. Now let us refocus and realize the diversity and attributes about '**The Godhead** you represent. **Acts 17:29, Rom. 1:20 and Col.2:9.**

The Full Nature and Characteristics of the GodHead

1	**God**	**Jesus Christ**	**Holy Spirit**
2	**Father**	**Son / Jesus**	**Spirit**
3	**Creator**	**Creator**	**Architect**
	Gen 1:1	**Gen. 1:26**	**Gen. 1:2**
4	**Lord**	**Lord**	**Lord**
5	**The Almighty**	**God/Mighty God**	**God**
	Gen. 17:1	**Isa. 9:6 / Rev. 1:8**	**Acts 5:3-4**
	--	--	--
6	**King & Judge**	**(King) of kings**	**Governor…Ps.22:28**
7	**Judge**	**Judge Matt. 5:22**	**Counselor John 14:26**
	In Hebrew He is:	**In Greek He is:**	**In Latin He is:**
8	**Elohim./ I am**	**Iesosus / I Am**	**Paraclete / I Am**
	Exodus 3:14	**Mark 14:62**	--
9	**Ab / Abba**	**Everlasting Father**	**Everlasting Comforter**
	Matt.28:19	**Isaiah 9:6**	**John 14:26, 16:13**
10	**God is Spirit**	**Word made flesh**	**Present everywhere**
	John 14:24	**John 1:1**	**Romans 8:9**
	--	--	--
11	**Love**	**Grace**	**Communion**
	II Cor. 13:14	**II Cor. 13:14**	**II Cor. 13:14**
12	**Operations**	**Administrations**	**Gifts**
	I Cor:12:4-6	**I Cor:12:4-6**	**I Cor:12:4-6**
13	**Teacher--I Thess. 4:9**	**Teacher--Jn. 8:20**	**Teacher--John 14:26**
14	**Giver—**	**Redeemer—**	**Sealer—**
	John 3:16	**Gal. 4:5**	**Eph. 1:13**
15	**Spirit of God**	**Spirit of Christ**	**Spirit of Truth**
	John 14:24	**Rom. 8:9**	**John 14:17**
16	**Provides a gift**	**Provides a gift**	**Provides a gift**
	John 3:16	**Acts 2:38**	**Acts 8:20**

AFC, Paul Vickers

Man's Three-fold Nature and Characteristics

1	Spirit (invisible)	Soul (mental)	Body (physical)
	Gen. 1:26	I Thes. 5:23	Heb. 4:12
2	Has to be…	Must Be…	Becomes the …
3	Born again	Rescued/saved	Temple /Holy Spirt
	John 3:3-5	Rom. 10:9-10	I Cor. 6:18
4	Perceives	Discern / learns	Senses the physical
	I Cor. 2:11	Matt12:30	I Cor. 6:13
5	Candle of The Lord	Most valuable asset	House spirit & soul
	Prov. 20:27	Matt. 16:26	Gen. 1:26
6	Returns to God…	Remains with us…	Returns to the dirt…
	at death of the body	for eternity	at death
	Ecc. 12:7	Gen.1:26/ Luke 16:23	Ecc. 12:7
7	Same outline as body	Determines final destiny	Eventually resurr'ctd
	II Cor. 12:2	Heb. 9:27	Jude 1:9, Mat. 22-33

The GodHead in a Condensed Capsule

1st. **God** called **Elohim** which is a plural Hebrew word and omniscient **G.O.D** is **G**enius **o**f **D**esign. **2nd**. **GOD** defined is = **Source/Sustainer**. **3rd.** **Jesus** is God's perfect revelation of Himself in the flesh. Hebr. 1:3 **4th**. **Jesus** is the **visible** image of the **invisible** God. Coll.1:15, He:

5th **J**oins----**6th**---**J**ustifies
Every------------**E**very
Sinner-----------**S**aint
Unto-------------**U**nto
Salvation--------**S**anctification

7th The **Holy Spirit** is the **One** and diverse person of the **Godhead**. Also, **He** is the **Power** of God, the **Spirit** of Christ and the **Revealer** of truth.

About the Author

Paul Vickers is an author and honorary graduate who has obtained his teacher's license from the Partners to The Promise –**PTP**– College of Christian Education and **The Trans-World Accrediting Commission International**. Paul will be obtaining another degree which is his Masters in June of 2020 as he continues to teach the young people about Godliness, finances and personal development. Paul wrote and published his first book in December 2015 which is entitled **"Understanding What Just Happened to You."** It spells out God's process of salvation in a comprehensive format. However, in 2019, Paul simplified his first work by putting out the "Second Edition" in December 2019.

Paul has recently completed a second book entitled, ***"The Acces$ible Economy of God,"*** It takes money *–our article of trade–* to a whole new level as he reveals God's four (4) financial instruments contained in His Word. The information it discloses will clarify for ministers, pastors and believers how money should be allocated personally and corporately within the body of Christ.

Finally, the current book you are reading is, ***"The Awesome Kingdom of God"*** sub-headed, '*In plain sight.*' He considers this his proudest work to date. All three books are available on Amazon.com. The eBook versions should all be available in January 2020. Finally, Paul is working on the audio version of all his Godly works to reach God's entire kingdom family across the globe. All books can be obtained on amazon.com/author/afcpaul

AFC, Paul Vickers

Made in the USA
Coppell, TX
19 December 2020